THINK BIG
TO WIN
BIG

By Darrin Donnelly

THINK LIKE A WARRIOR
The Five Inner Beliefs That Make You Unstoppable

OLD SCHOOL GRIT
Times May Change, But the Rules for Success Never Do

RELENTLESS OPTIMISM
How a Commitment to Positive Thinking Changes Everything

LIFE TO THE FULLEST
A Story About Finding Your Purpose and Following Your Heart

VICTORY FAVORS THE FEARLESS
How to Defeat the 7 Fears That Hold You Back

THE TURNAROUND
How to Build Life-Changing Confidence

THE MENTAL GAME
Winning the War Within Your Mind

THINK BIG TO WIN BIG
The Bigger You Believe, The Bigger You Achieve

THINK BIG TO WIN BIG

THE BIGGER YOU BELIEVE
THE BIGGER YOU ACHIEVE

Darrin Donnelly

Cover design: Damonza
Cover images: Shutterstock

ISBN: 979-8-9880102-1-0

Library of Congress Control Number available upon request.

Visit us at: SportsForTheSoul.com

Sports for the Soul ®

Books That Motivate, Inspire, and Empower.

This book is part of the *Sports for the Soul* series. For updates on this book, future books, and a free newsletter that delivers advice and inspiration from top coaches, athletes, and sports psychologists, join us at: **SportsForTheSoul.com**.

The *Sports for the Soul* newsletter will help you:

- Find your calling and follow your passion
- Harness the power of positive thinking
- Build your self-confidence
- Attack every day with joy and enthusiasm
- Develop mental toughness
- Increase your energy and stay motivated
- Explore the spiritual side of success
- Be a positive leader for your family and your team
- And much more…

Join us at: **SportsForTheSoul.com**.

To Laura, Patrick, Katie, and Tommy;

who are everything to me.

Introduction

Study the top leaders and achievers in any field—in business, in sales, in sports, in virtually any profession—and you will find there is one trait above all others that separates them from their competition.

The top achievers think *bigger* than everyone else.

They have big goals, big dreams, and big expectations for what they can achieve. They expect big results and they live up to those expectations.

Whether we realize it or not, most of us are limiting ourselves—professionally, financially, physically, and mentally—by thinking too small. This is because we all live up to (or down to) our expectations.

If you're not thinking big enough about what you want out of life and what you can achieve, you will never live up to your full potential.

Great achievers think *bigger*. They think big about their future, always enthusiastic about what's ahead. They set big, exciting goals and they *expect* to achieve them. They have a big, positive vision for what life can look like and they *expect* to get there.

When you start thinking bigger, something amazing happens. Life starts meeting you at your new level of thinking. When you have a bigger, more positive vision of your future, you start experiencing a bigger, more positive life.

This book is about shifting your mindset to think bigger.

In this motivational fable, Sean Riley is a freelance sportswriter struggling to find steady work. Once an ambitious man with big dreams and goals, Sean has grown frustrated with his life and adopted a limited, cynical outlook about what he's capable of.

But Sean gets a golden opportunity when he's hired to write a feature story on Jay Porter, the unconventional NFL coach who has led his underdog team to the Super Bowl. The two weeks Sean spends with Coach Porter in the leadup to the Super Bowl will be two weeks that completely change his outlook on life.

As this story plays out, Sean learns the principles that separate big thinkers and big achievers from everyone else.

- Big thinkers believe success is a choice, determined by the size of one's vision and their commitment to that vision. Small thinkers believe success is determined by lucky breaks.

- Big thinkers dare to dream big and aren't afraid to take bold risks. Small thinkers play it too safe and fear what might happen if they aim too high.

- Big thinkers attach themselves to a bigger purpose and make short-term sacrifices to achieve a long-term vision. Small thinkers focus on "what's in it for me" in the short term instead of what they can contribute to the larger objective.

- Big thinkers believe they are bigger than their problems. They rely on big passion and enthusiasm to power through adversity. Small thinkers get easily stressed out when facing adversity and allow short-term defeats to derail them.

- Big thinkers adopt a growth mindset and are constantly adapting to changing conditions while chasing bigger levels of success. Small thinkers fear change and are always looking for ways to coast and maintain.

- Big thinkers look beyond temporary setbacks and stay focused on the things they can control. Small thinkers worry constantly about everything that could go wrong and obsess over the things they can't control.

- Big thinkers have a big, optimistic vision for the future. Small thinkers think it's naive to be optimistic and tend to live in the past.

In this book, you will see how simple shifts in your thinking can lead you to new levels of success. You will learn how to break through the common, limiting beliefs that hold you back from reaching your full potential. You will discover how the size of your thinking ultimately determines the size of your success.

The size of your thinking affects every area of your life: your finances, your relationships, your physical health, your mental health, and your peace of mind. **The bigger you think, the more successful you will be.**

It's time to start thinking bigger and reaching new levels of success in *every* area of your life!

Darrin Donnelly
SportsForTheSoul.com

"To be an overachiever,
you have to be an over-believer."
- DABO SWINNEY

Two-Time National Champion College Football Coach

1

This is not the story I intended to write. It's certainly not the story I was hired to write. But it is the story I *had* to write.

This book will set the record straight about what happened when I spent two weeks with Coach Jay Porter and his team as they prepared to play in the Super Bowl. Two weeks that would change my life in ways I was completely unprepared for.

I know, I know. It sounds like hyperbole to claim one's life can be dramatically changed in just two weeks. But that's what happened to me.

What started as a dream assignment for this not-so-young sportswriter became much more than an inside look at how an underdog pro football team prepares for the biggest game of their lives, which is the story I was hired to write. Instead, it became something closer to a two-week coaching session that forced me to question many of my core beliefs—beliefs I would learn were holding me back from a happy and successful life. It became a master class on how the thoughts we choose to think impact *everything* we experience. And it became an invitation to turn my life around by changing the way I thought.

If you had told me prior to those two weeks that I had the power to achieve just about anything I put my mind to, I would have rolled my eyes and laughed. I was way too smart—and too jaded by my own experiences—to fall for such naive promises.

Sure, I wasn't happy with my life, but I was content with believing my failures and my unhappiness were not *my* fault. Life just happened to us and I had been dealt a bad hand. Nothing I could do about it except try to survive and hope my luck would someday turn.

That's the way I thought. That's how I viewed the world *before* I met an unconventional football coach named Jay Porter.

But I'm getting ahead of myself.

I suppose the best place to start this story is the night of the NFC Championship Game. The St. Louis Stallions—an NFL expansion team less than a decade old—were down by 10 points with four minutes left to play. It looked like the Los Angeles Rams were going to end the underdog story that had captivated the football world for the last month.

The Stallions, led by their eccentric second-year head coach, had caught fire after a 5–8 start to the season. They won their final four games of the regular season, two of those in overtime, to somehow win the watered-down NFC South Division title and earn a playoff spot with a 9–8 record.

As underdogs, the Stallions came from behind to win their first two playoff games. Now, they were playing in the NFC Championship against a heavily favored Rams team that expected to be playing in another hometown Super Bowl.

The NFC Championship was being played in L.A., the city that would also be hosting this year's Super Bowl. I happened to be a sportswriter living in L.A. So naturally, I was taking in all the action from inside the press box at the luxurious SoFi Stadium, right?

Not exactly.

Though I still identified myself as a sportswriter when asked, it had been years since my name, Sean Riley, had regularly bylined articles in the sports section of the *L.A. Herald*. That, of course, was because the *L.A. Herald* no longer existed.

These days, I was freelancing. Begging online sports sites to publish my work. I'd get articles published here and there, but the work was far from steady and even farther from lucrative. In fact, it had been three months since I had last been paid for an article.

What was I doing during the Sunday night of the NFC Championship Game hosted in my home city? Mostly driving people all over L.A. as an Uber driver.

I was driving a passenger home from the airport when the Stallions' quarterback, Troy Wallace, broke free on a fourth-and-five scramble that turned into a 42-yard touchdown run to close the St. Louis deficit to 3 points with three-and-a-half minutes left to play. I was driving a different passenger to a restaurant when L.A. missed a field goal with 57 seconds left in the game. And I was sitting outside of a sports bar waiting for another passenger when the radio announcers said St. Louis Head Coach Jay Porter, with five seconds left in the game, had decided to go for the win from 3 yards out instead of kicking the game-tying field goal that would have sent the game to overtime.

I got out of my car and hurried into the sports bar

to watch the final play of the game. Wallace faked the give to running back Jaylin Mack before throwing the perfect touch pass to a wide open, 6-foot-6, 315-pound offensive tackle for the game-winning touchdown.

The sports bar erupted with anger.

"He can't do that!"

"That's an ineligible receiver!"

"Illegal. Completely illegal!"

I knew right away the play was legal. And brilliant.

The Stallions had used the old tackle-eligible play to win their seventh game in a row and punch their ticket to the Super Bowl. The legend of Jay Porter, the kooky college coach that everybody thought St. Louis was crazy to hire two years ago, would continue growing for at least another two weeks.

"You've got to be kidding me," I said to no one in particular. "What a Bush League call." My way of trying to degrade what I knew was actually an outstanding call that had stunned the Rams and all of their fans.

What else could I say?

Jay Porter and his St. Louis Stallions had just shocked the sports world by beating another team they had no business beating. The Los Angeles Rams *deserved* to be playing in the Super Bowl. They were *destined* to play in a Super Bowl hosted in their own city. My city. My team.

Coach Porter and his upstart St. Louis Stallions had ruined it for all of us.

2

I spent the rest of the evening giving rides to patrons who had mostly overindulged at local establishments following the game. And they were not happy.

"How did the refs allow that? They never declared the guy eligible."

"How did our coaching staff not see that coming? Where's the preparation? Heads need to roll."

"How do you blow a lead like that?"

"What a joke this team is. Losing to a clown show like St. Louis."

I heard comments like that all through the night. And I shared their anger.

This was not a good time for me to be experiencing any more disappointment. Ever since I lost my job with the *Herald* almost three years ago, I had been struggling through life.

Three years. Had it been that long?

When I was hired by the *L.A. Herald* two years after

college, it was a dream come true. Jenny and I were newlyweds from Iowa. I was hired to write for the sports page of the city's second-largest newspaper and Jenny was accepted by UCLA's doctorate program to pursue her goal of becoming a math professor. We arrived in January, leaving the bitter cold of a Midwest winter behind for the blue skies and bright sunshine of Southern California.

We were starting the careers we'd dreamed of. We would soon be starting our family. We were so excited about the future.

Those exciting days now felt like another lifetime. When I thought back on them, it was like I was observing old acquaintances I no longer kept in touch with. Idealistic, naive dreamers who should've known better about what awaited them. Barely-recognizable kids blinded by youthful enthusiasm, not realizing how quickly the harsh realities of adulthood were about to smack them in the face.

For eight years, I worked my way up from the high school sports beat to the college beat to the NFL beat. My goal was to become a sports columnist for the *Herald*, eventually parlaying that into a national sports columnist gig, ideally at a much larger publication.

During this time, I also worked on a few book ideas, even a few screenplay ideas. I wanted to be like those great sportswriters I'd grown up reading. My heroes. Guys who wrote columns and insider stories for publications like *Sports Illustrated* and published bestselling sports books, some of which became movies.

That was the life I wanted. And everything was headed in that direction.

Until it wasn't.

I should have seen it coming sooner. The *Herald* started eliminating pages, some staff, then full sections of the paper, then more staff. Before I knew it, moving *up* was no longer my goal, I just wanted to stay *on*.

I did hang on until the end, mostly because the *Herald* didn't need to pay me as much as the veteran writers they had on the staff. But the end came nonetheless.

After the third or fourth time a larger company supposedly changed its mind about buying the paper, the *Herald* finally closed its doors for good and I was out of a job.

The timing could not have been worse. The entire

newspaper industry was struggling and the papers that survived weren't looking to expand their staffs. Just like that, my big dreams were vanishing.

I spent my first year of unemployment firing out resumes to every newspaper within driving distance. I called up editors and offered to work longer hours for less pay. It made no difference. Nobody was hiring and the reporters that still had jobs were clinging to them for dear life.

I started targeting online sports sites. Aiming for fulltime positions, but offering to do freelance work. I got hired to write articles here and there, but the pay was low and inconsistent.

I stopped working on books after I lost my job. I felt it would be irresponsible to spend time chasing big dreams like that when I should be focusing on finding a regular job.

Jenny and I survived. I joined the gig economy, picking up odd jobs that mostly resolved around giving people rides as an Uber driver or delivering people food as a DoorDasher. We now had two kids and somehow managed to hold on to the small home we bought five years into my job with the *Herald*. But every month was a struggle, with no signs of that struggle ending anytime soon.

As I drove passengers through Los Angeles late into Sunday night, I thought about how thrilled I was when we first moved here, and how I now wished we had never come. The sights and sounds of this city that once inspired me now served as constant reminders of the big dreams I would never achieve.

L.A. is such an exciting place to be when you're in your mid-twenties, starting your professional life with all your hopes and dreams in front of you. It's the place where ambitious twentysomethings from all over the nation have been flocking to for more than a century to chase their biggest fantasies about what life could be. It's Hollywood, after all, the place where wild fantasies are created and distributed to the rest of the world.

L.A. is not such an exciting place to be when you're an unemployed thirtysomething who can't catch a break and it seems like everyone else your age has struck their gold, or at least settled into comfortable silver or bronze positions. When it seems like nothing is going your way, you start to resent all the starry-eyed dreamers you encounter in this city. They show up thinking they're going to overcome the odds and become famous actors, writers, musicians, and entrepreneurs. Who do they think they are, expecting *their* dreams to come true?

When you're struggling in this town, even the sunshine and beaches can feel like they're mocking you for thinking you just might have what it takes to make it here.

I suppose those feelings are similar no matter where you live. When life is going well, you look around and notice all kinds of things to be grateful for. When life is going bad, you look around and feel as though everyone has it made except for you. At least, that's how I felt for the three years I spent begging for work after the *Herald* closed its doors.

3

When I finally got home from driving passengers all over the city on the night of the NFC Championship, it was nearly two in the morning. I was exhausted and still stewing about the game. I knew it was "just a game" and I was far from being an L.A. Rams superfan, but in my current state even the littlest disappointment could feel like another punch to the gut. Yet another frustration thrown onto the pile of frustrations my life had become. Yet another thing to be angry about. Yet another thing to feel sorry for myself about.

Can anything go right for me?

I checked in on my six-year-old son, James, and my eight-year-old daughter, Ellie, both sleeping peacefully in their beds. Seeing them sleep made me feel overwhelmed with love … but also overwhelmed with guilt, like I was letting them down for not providing a better life—the life these two sweet kids deserved. Their friends at school all had dads who had their lives figured out. They were professionals, working their way up in responsible careers. They were earning good livings, providing for their families, scoring promotions at work.

And here I was, in my mid-thirties, driving drunks home from the bars until two in the morning. *This* is what I was doing with my life.

Those feelings didn't go away when I opened my bedroom door and saw my wife, Jenny, sleeping soundly. She was now an Assistant Professor at Loyola Marymount, a small college here in L.A. She too had her life together. She was moving up, following her dream, earning a good salary for us while still raising two wonderful kids. She was doing her part. What was I contributing to this family?

Though Jenny never voiced any resentment about me falling short—*way* short—of my career goals, it was moments like this where I would compare our roles in this family and feel like a total failure. She was doing what working adults were supposed to be doing at this hour—resting up for a day of work in a career she enjoyed and was excelling at. I was living more like the college students she taught—still up past two in the morning, working a gig that didn't require any expertise besides knowing how to drive a car and listen to a GPS voice. Of course, college kids doing this sort of work still had their whole lives in front of them. They were working towards exciting futures. I felt like my life was behind me, and I wondered how I had missed my calling so badly.

This isn't the way it's supposed to be, I thought to myself.

I laid down next to Jenny. She turned over and grabbed my hand.

"Glad your home," she whispered with a smile, her eyes still closed.

"Me too," I said as I squeezed her hand. I was trying hard not to give any indication of how angry I was at the moment.

I wasn't angry at her, of course. I wasn't even that angry about the game. I was angry at myself. *Why couldn't I get my life together?*

After an hour or so of tossing and turning, my mind racing no matter how much I tried to calm it, I decided to step outside for some fresh air. (One thing I always appreciated about living in L.A. was being able to step outside in the middle of a January night and not freeze to death.)

I opened the sliding glass door and stepped out to the back patio of the home we could barely afford thanks to my lackluster earnings.

I took a few deep breaths and looked up at the night sky. *Where did I go wrong?*

Not even a minute after I had stepped outside, I heard the door slide open behind me. Jenny had come to check on me.

"What are you doing out here?" she said.

"Just getting some fresh air."

She wrapped her arms around me and hugged me tight, resting her head on my chest. "Upset about the game?"

"You saw it?"

"I did," she said. "What a bummer. That would've been exciting for the city."

We stood together in silence. I didn't want to tell her what was actually on my mind. I had been struggling with these feelings of frustration and inadequacy for months now, trying to hold it together without having some kind of mental meltdown.

"Why don't you come to bed?" she said.

"I can't sleep," I said.

"Sean, I can't sleep as well when you're not with me. Makes me worry about you."

I let that statement linger in the night air for a moment before asking her the question on my mind. "Have you thought anymore about what we talked about?"

She pulled her head away from my chest and looked up at me.

"What did we talk about?"

"About moving," I said. "Going back home. Back to Iowa."

She wrinkled her eyebrows, giving me a look that said she wasn't quite sure what I was talking about.

"Remember?' I said. "At Christmas, when we were back home? We both said what a nice time we had. How we missed it."

"Oh, right," she said, placing her head back on my chest. "I guess I thought we were just being—you know—nostalgic."

"I wasn't."

She went upright and pulled away from me just a bit. No longer hugging me, her hands now holding my wrists.

"You want to move back to Iowa?" she said.

"I've been thinking about it a lot. Things are obviously not working for me here. Do you realize it's been three years since I had a regular-paying writing job? *Three years* and I'm no closer to lining up a steady paycheck. You know what's happened to the newspaper business. Those jobs are gone and they're not coming back. I think it's time to face reality."

Jenny stepped back and tightened her robe to stay warm. She tilted her head to the side. She hadn't expected this middle-of-the-night conversation. "You're still freelancing. One of those sites will eventually bring you on fulltime."

"They haven't yet," I said, stating the obvious. "And the freelance work isn't exactly paying the bills. Which is another reason I think we should consider moving. If I'm going to keep freelancing, it only makes sense to live somewhere that costs a lot less to live, right?"

"I don't understand where this is coming from. Last week, you said you had some new ideas you were excited about."

I exhaled. It was time to come clean.

"Jenny, I'm just trying to keep a positive face. Truth

is, I've got nothing in the tank. I'm blocked. I'm so angry about where I am, I can't think straight. All the rejection finally broke me. I feel like life is trying to tell me it's time for a change."

Her eyes glistened. It was breaking her heart to hear this.

"But the kids, they love their school and their friends. And I'm on track to becoming full Professor at a college I love. This is our life now. I love where we're from and I miss family and old friends too, but we've built our lives *here*."

"I know … *you're* doing great here." I realized how selfish I sounded, but I continued. "I'm proud of everything you're doing, but I don't know what I'm doing with *my* life. I know I sound self-centered, but I keep thinking about what life would be like for us if we had never come out here in the first place. I look at my little brother. You've seen his house. He's crushing it back home."

"You want to be a dentist, now?"

"No, I'm just saying, he's doing well. Really well. We could be doing something like that. My buddy, Pete, he's in Des Moines, just killing it in sales, making a fortune. I talked to him not long ago, he told me he could get me a job with his company if I wanted."

"You don't want to be a writer anymore?"

"Not if it means living like this. Look, I gave it a shot. It didn't work out. It's time for me to take the hint. It's not the career I'm cut out for."

Jenny rubbed her eyes. "It's late. You had a bad day. I think you'll feel different in the morning."

"I won't," I said. "I've been thinking about this for a long time."

"You're serious?"

"I am."

Jenny looked down, disappointed to hear my answer.

After a long pause, she said, "Remember when we first moved out here? We were so excited. *You* were so excited. You had such big dreams. You were going to become a national columnist and write books. You were so convinced you could do it. And so was I. Sean, you *can* still do those things. I thought you still wanted to. What happened?"

I sighed. "Reality happened."

4

By the time I woke up the next morning, Jenny was already at work and the kids were at school. It must have been five in the morning before I finally fell asleep the night before. It was nearly noon now. Sleeping until noon on a weekday only reinforced my feelings of inadequacy, like a slacker who couldn't get his life together.

But on this morning, my life was about to change. Why does that happen? Right when you think things are only getting worse and are never going to change, you catch a break that shifts your trajectory. This was one of those much-needed breaks.

When I grabbed my phone, I saw that I had missed a call from Ethan Grover. A jolt of excitement shot through me.

Ethan was the very-hands-on co-founder and national editor of a sports site called *The Cheap Seats*. It had started as a two-man blog called *A View from the*

Cheap Seats, but over the last six years had grown into a nationally-recognized site.

The Cheap Seats was one of those irreverent sports sites that was especially popular with younger readers. They loved to publish wild rumors, controversial opinions, and video clips recorded by fans at sporting events showing other fans behaving badly. *The Cheap Seats* specialized in sports-based clickbait.

Amidst all the attention-garnering headlines, the site also published some more traditional sports pieces. They had some thoughtful content, you just had to dig around to find it. A few of their columnists and reporters even sounded like actual journalists, though they were mostly overshadowed by the more controversial material the site was known for.

As a freelancer, I had published a handful of articles with *The Cheap Seats* over the last couple of years. My articles were more traditional in nature and therefore didn't generate the type of traffic Ethan and the gang were looking for. I didn't receive a response to my last few emails pitching ideas or asking for opportunities. That's why seeing Ethan's name as a missed call made me immediately dial him back, hoping he had an assignment for me.

"Sean, this is Ethan," he said after one ring, as though we were longtime buddies on a first-name basis. "You live in L.A., right?"

"Yes, I do. Tough morning around here."

"I bet, but what a game. Listen, I think I have the perfect job for you if you're interested."

I had only spoken with Ethan once before, when he called with a last-minute question about an article I wrote. I didn't know him well, but I had listened to his podcast and seen him on TV plenty of times. He was witty and had a likeable personality, one of those back-slapping, never-met-a-stranger kind of guys. But he also liked to spark controversy and, in my opinion, would sometimes cross the line in order to drum up attention for his brand. I had heard stories about how you didn't want to get on his bad side; he knew how to hold a grudge.

Right now, I was talking with the personable and charming version of Ethan.

"I'm *definitely* interested," I said.

"You're not going to believe this, but I just had my main West Coast writer quit on me. I think he's moving to Fox Sports. You believe that? He's been writing for us for four years and two weeks before the Super Bowl, the dude just up and leaves. No warning. No nothing. Not very professional, if you ask me."

I fought the urge to point out that *The Cheap Seats* hadn't exactly garnered a reputation for *professional* journalism over the years.

"But hey, I don't want to bash the guy," Ethan said. "I'm sure he had his reasons. The problem is, he was my L.A. guy. And with the Super Bowl there in L.A., we need somebody to fill in, like *immediately*, for what he was working on. I was thinking about writers I admired out there and I remembered how much I loved that piece you wrote for us about the Pac-12 falling apart. You got great quotes from A.D.s and coaches. I thought to myself, 'This guy gets it. We need more articles from him.'"

I almost pointed out that I had sent over several ideas since my last published article, but nobody from *The Cheap Seats* had responded to my emails.

Ethan continued. "So here I am, I just lost my L.A. guy, hotel rooms are going through the roof for the Super Bowl, and I'm thinking, 'Sean Riley lives out there and he would be the perfect guy for this story.'"

"I really appreciate that," I said, skeptical if Ethan's

glowing admiration for my work was authentic, but enjoying it nonetheless.

"It's a big story. A two-week assignment. If all goes well with it, we'd probably bring you on fulltime. You want the gig?"

"Absolutely," I said, not sure what the gig was.

"Great! How fast can you get to St. Louis?"

5

Ethan explained how he had personally worked out a deal to have one of his writers spend the two weeks leading up to the Super Bowl with Jay Porter and his St. Louis Stallions. The deal had been in place for weeks. If the Stallions somehow made it to the Super Bowl, the writer would get some exclusive access to Porter and his squad leading up to the nation's biggest sporting event. It was a longshot that paid off.

So why was the other writer leaving right before such a great opportunity? Ethan didn't go into details and I'm sure there was more to the story, but it sounded like the writer was using the exclusive access as a negotiation tactic: give me a raise before I start the story or I'm gone. Ethan called his bluff and lost.

Regardless of what all went down with the previous writer, Ethan now had to bring in a new writer for the job. That writer, it turned out, would be me.

The plan was for me to spend a couple of days with the team this week in St. Louis. Then, when the team flew to L.A. next week, I'd be able to follow them and Ethan wouldn't have to shell out any extra money for hotel stays during the expensive Super Bowl week since I was already living in L.A.

In other words, despite Ethan's flattery, which I certainly appreciated hearing, I knew the main reason Ethan was offering me this gig was not because I was some great writer whose style he thought would be perfect for the feature, but because I happened to live in L.A. and could save him big bucks by commuting to and from the team's Super Bowl training facility.

As they say, sometimes it's better to be lucky than good. I was due for a lucky break and I jumped at the opportunity.

Though, there was one caveat.

"Sean, there is one thing I want you to keep in mind with this story," Ethan said before ending our call. "As much as I appreciate the access we're being granted, I don't want this to be a puff piece. Everybody is gushing over this Porter guy and there are going to be a million Cinderella stories written about this team. I don't want that to be us. We have to be different.

"This feature is going to go live the night before the Super Bowl and I want America to be talking about it. I want it to be something everyone is talking about *during* the Super Bowl. You can't buy publicity like that. I want this to be big. *Really* big. Do you understand what I'm saying?"

"You want me to find something that will make headlines, something … *controversial* about Porter?"

"It doesn't have to be salacious, but I want you to dig deep. I want you to find something that shows how this guy isn't the folk hero everyone else is making him out to be. You've seen him on TV. You've heard his interviews, all those hokey lines he drops and that *Think Big to Win Big* schtick of his. I know he's a likeable guy. Hell, I like him too. But likeable profiles don't sell. We need to be different. We need to stand out. While everyone else is saying what a great guy he is, I want to reveal what he really is."

I paused before asking, "What is he?"

"In my opinion, a glorified gym teacher who stumbled his way into this job and happens to be on the luckiest streak in NFL history."

6

During my redeye flight to St. Louis—a flight Ethan promised he'd reimburse me for—I kept replaying parts of my conversation with Ethan.

Mostly, I was thrilled with the opportunity. I felt like my luck might *finally* be turning. Here I was being offered two weeks' pay to cover the hottest team in America before the biggest game in the world. I was being handed a sportswriter's dream assignment, which would include a press pass to the Super Bowl. On top of it all, Ethan told me if I came through for him on this story, it would likely lead to a fulltime job with *The Cheap Seats*.

For those reasons, I was ecstatic during my flight.

But I also had a slight feeling of trepidation. I wasn't crazy about the tone of the article Ethan was looking for. From everything I had seen and heard about Jay Porter, I found his gung-ho, fun-loving approach to the game refreshing. The NFL had plenty of coaches who said little and wore their stress like a badge of honor. Coach Porter spoke so freely that his press conferences would frequently veer off into subjects that had nothing to do with football. He was sometimes laughed at by reporters for what they called "silly" or "Pollyannish" comments, but nobody was laughing now. He had his team in the Super Bowl.

Like most other fans and media members, I couldn't help but root for a guy like Jay Porter. Did I want to be the sportswriter who spent two weeks with him and then blindsided him with a hit piece on Super Bowl morning?

Plus, as much as I needed a job, was a site like *The Cheap Seats*, which specialized in controversy and clickbait, where I wanted to write fulltime?

Beggars can't be choosers. What choice did I have? I was in no position to turn down an offer like this.

Who knows? I thought to myself. *Maybe Ethan is right and there is a dark side to Jay Porter that needs to be exposed. What do I really know about how he treats his players? We only see the side of him he allows the media to see at press conferences. I'm a journalist. It's my job to find out such things.*

Bottom line is that after seeing how excited Jenny

was when I told her about this lucky break, there was no way I was going to turn this opportunity down. Finally, I had something to be excited about. Something to look forward to. I couldn't wait to meet this Jay Porter guy and see what he was like behind the scenes.

7

Tuesday morning, I drove my rental car to STLHQ, the extravagant campus that served as the St. Louis franchise's headquarters and training facilities. The billionaire who owned this still-young expansion team had spared no expense to bring pro football back to St. Louis.

The campus of fresh, clean buildings and meticulously kept landscapes and practice fields were impressive. I had been to a few other team headquarters during my time with the *L.A. Herald* and despite being organizations worth billions of dollars, you'd be surprised at how mediocre some of those facilities were. That was not the case here. Everything looked brand new and first class.

After working my way through security checkpoints and finding my way around the campus, I finally made it to Coach Porter's office ten minutes before noon, which is when we were scheduled to meet.

"Go on in, he's expecting you," his secretary told me after I introduced myself.

His office door was slightly ajar. I knocked quietly as I opened the door wider and leaned in to see Porter reclining back and facing a huge TV screen behind his desk. He was reviewing film. Stopping, starting, rewinding, moving forward frame by frame. He must not have heard me. He was focused on his film study and I worried I might be intruding.

"Uh, Coach Porter?" I said, knocking again, this time a little louder.

"Yeah?" he said, not looking back.

I entered the spacious office and closed the door behind me. "I'm sorry to interrupt. My name is Sean Riley. I'm a writer for *The Cheap Seats.*"

"Yeah, yeah, come on in, have a seat."

With his remote, he moved the frame on the screen forward again, his eyes still locked on the screen. He was going over and over the few frames right after the snap of the ball in the Cincinnati-Buffalo playoff game from a week ago. Forward a few frames, then back, then forward again. He was looking for something. A tendency, I assumed, but I wasn't exactly sure.

He made a quick note on the notepad he was holding, then swung around to greet me, the big screen behind his desk now paused.

"That's a helluva team were getting ready for," he said, pointing with his thumb to the screen behind him.

I nodded. "They've got some serious talent."

That was an understatement. St. Louis would be facing the Cincinnati Bengals in the Super Bowl. The Bengals, who had only lost one game this season, were favored by 17.5 points, the second-largest pregame point spread in Super Bowl history. Not since 1995, when the 49ers were favored by 18.5 points, had a Super Bowl point spread been so large. The 49ers won that game by 23 points.

"So where you from, Sean?"

Coach Porter was wearing a gray t-shirt and a blue and silver ballcap, both displaying the same *STL* logo that graced the Stallions' team helmets. He had a tendency to adjust his cap up-and-down often, almost like he was scratching his forehead with it.

"Iowa, originally. I live in L.A. now."

"That had to be a culture shock," he said with a smile.

"It was. Still is, actually."

"You a Clone or a Hawkeye?" He was referring to Iowa's two major universities, the Iowa Hawkeyes and the Iowa State Cyclones.

"Clones, all the way. I'm an Iowa State grad."

"That's a good school, always loved their fans. And that grass field of theirs. I don't know if there's a better-quality grass field in all of college football. I love that they still play on grass, especially in the cold like they are."

"The school is very proud of that grass," I said. And then we proceeded to have a ten-minute conversation about maintaining grass in cold weather and the debate over artificial turf versus natural grass playing surfaces. (For the record, Coach Porter preferred playing on grass.)

This is the type of thing Coach Porter had become somewhat famous for at his press conferences. Something mentioned would catch his attention, football-related or not, and he would start an in-depth conversation about the topic. It would often get to the point where he was asking reporters more questions than they were asking him. The man was perpetually curious. And it wasn't an act reserved for when the cameras were rolling, as I was seeing now and would see often in the two weeks to come.

I enjoyed his genuine interest in topics outside of football just as much as when he'd rant about the game he loved. The only problem was finding the best way to transition back to the subject I was being paid to gather information about. Most times, I would simply wait for him to shift the topic for us, which is what he abruptly did after the topic of grass and winter fertilization had run its course.

"So you're here to write about what we're doing to get ready for the Super Bowl, right?" he said.

"Exactly, Coach, and I'd like to get to know more about you and your philosophy along the way."

"Call me Jay," he said.

"You got it."

"What happened to the other guy? Ethan said he left your outfit?"

"Yeah, I really don't know what happened. But I'm thrilled for this opportunity."

"You seem like a good dude, Sean. I think this will work just fine. All I ask is, like I told Ethan, nothing gets printed before the Super Bowl that could give Cincy an edge on us. I don't want anything you see about our prep hurting us in the game. Nothing about specific plays were working on or tendencies we're game-planning for. If you want to print that stuff, I ask that you do it after the game. We on the same page?"

"Of course," I said, making a mental note that perhaps I could string this assignment out to a few postgame stories as well.

"Also, I'm an open book," Jay said. "I've got nothing to hide. I'll own what I say and what I do. I only ask that you cover everything as is and don't try to stir something up that isn't there. I know the kind of stuff *The Cheap Seats* likes to post. Ethan swears this feature is part of his effort to change their image and I'm happy to help with that. But I'll be honest, I'm not sure I completely trust Ethan."

I repositioned myself in my seat. "You can trust me. I won't print anything that isn't fact."

"Good deal."

Jay stood up and extended his hand. I did the same and shook his firm grip.

I hoped I had not made a promise I couldn't keep.

8

I spent most of Tuesday sitting in on coaches' meetings, listening and taking notes, trying not to be a nuisance. The coaches were putting together their game plan for Cincinnati. Even though this was technically a bye week and the Super Bowl was two Sundays away, Jay told me he wanted to make sure they had a good week of practice this week since there would be so many distractions once they got to L.A. next week.

Late in the afternoon, the Stallions had a team meeting with the players. They went over the upcoming itinerary, travel, and ticket details that would be unique for the Super Bowl. Then their head coach took to the stage and talked about the importance of maintaining their regular routines, staying mentally focused, and not letting any so-called *Super Bowl hype* rattle them.

The goal, he said, was to treat this game the same

way they treated every other game. The St. Louis coaches had apparently made it a point all season long to treat *every* game like it was the biggest game of the season. Treating the Super Bowl like the biggest game of the year, which it undeniably *was*, would be no different than the way they treated all their previous games. That was the hope, at least.

"Men, this is where we expected to be when we started this season," Jay said, as he addressed the auditorium-like meeting room. "You've got to think big to win big. That's been our message from the start. No one in this room should be surprised we're about to play in the biggest game there is. I sure as hell am not. This is where we envisioned ourselves being way back in July when we started training camp. I said it then, I've said it often, and I'll keep saying it: **the bigger you believe, the bigger you achieve**. Thinking big means *expecting* to play in big games and competing on the biggest stage. You believed you could get here, you envisioned yourself getting here, and now you're here. That's not an accident."

It was those type of lines that made me suppress a cynical eye roll. Talk like that was why some fans and media members didn't think Coach Porter belonged in the NFL. They viewed him as a rah-rah type of coach who was all hype, a former meathead fullback who was more motivational speaker than football coach.

From the moment he was hired, skeptics said his style and his message might have worked in college, but it wouldn't work in the NFL, where you're no longer leading impressionable young men. In this league, you're asked to lead well-paid, sometimes-jaded, business-minded adults who could see right past goofy motivational gimmicks. According to the skeptics in the media, that was why so few successful college coaches had the same level of success in the pros.

But as Jay spoke to his team, I looked around and noticed his players were locked in on every word. To them, his message wasn't a show; it wasn't a gimmick. I didn't see any players rolling their eyes or nudging the player next to them or smirking at each other. As far as I could tell, these players believed Jay Porter and they were buying his message.

Maybe it was because the proof was in the pudding. After all, huge underdog or not, this team *was* about to play in the Super Bowl. Any doubters in this group back when the team was 5–8 would likely have become converted believers by now.

Or maybe they had been buying into his message from day one because they saw him as one of their own. In his mid-fifties now, Jay still had the imposing athletic build that once made him a feared fullback at Texas A&M back in the 1990s. Sort of like the grizzled general who had the battle scars to prove he could be trusted by his soldiers, Jay looked like he just might have a few snaps left in him.

Maybe it was the passion he exuded. Despite two seasons of pro ball in Canada and invitations to three NFL training camps in three years, Jay Porter never did make an NFL roster. He now saw himself in every player in that meeting room. He shared their desire to make it in this league. To make it *big* in this league. He wanted them to make the most of the opportunity he never got. He had a fire in him and the players could feel it. So could I.

"Thirty-two other teams wish they were in your shoes right now," Jay told the team. "You've earned the right to be here and you should be proud of yourselves. But our job isn't done yet.

"Every week, our goal is the same: one-and-oh.

Doesn't matter what happened the week before or what might happen weeks down the line. We are focused on only the task right in front of us. All year long, I've told you the game we're about to play is the biggest game of the season because it's the only game you're guaranteed. That philosophy doesn't change with this game. The goal is still the same. What it will take to achieve that goal is still the same.

"Throughout the history of the NFL, a lot of teams have made it to the Super Bowl and then buckled to the pressure and the hype. The game was too big for them. That's not us.

"Everything we've always done is on a big scale. It has been all season long. We think big, we lift big, we prepare big, we hit big, we play big. We rise to the biggest moments because that is how we think, that is what we do, and that is *who we are*. We were made for this game. It's too big for most people, but not for you because you've trained yourselves to think big and win big.

"The fact that we're in this game when nobody outside this room thought we had a chance to be here is proof that **the size of your thinking determines the size of your success**.

"Like I've always said, everybody in this league does similar things to get physically prepared for their next game. Everybody does similar things to make sure they're mentally and schematically ready to do the things that need to be done on Sunday. The difference maker is the attitude you bring to the game. Attitude is the way you choose to think. The *size* of your thinking makes the difference.

"The key over the next two weeks is to keep doing the things that got you to this point. **Keep thinking big, preparing big, and expecting big things to happen for you.** If you keep doing that, you're going to keep shocking the world."

Think Big to Win Big.

That was Coach Porter's motto. It was painted in huge letters on the wall behind the main stage in the team meeting room. It was painted in the hallways throughout the facilities. It was painted on the weight-room walls and displayed on two enormous banners hung inside the team's indoor practice facility. It was displayed on a plaque that sat on his office desk and, yes, it was painted on his office wall. Jay Porter included the message with every fan autograph he signed. You couldn't get away from his message.

He had brought the message with him from his days as a college coach and skeptics criticized it as over-branding. Was he trying to motivate his team or promote himself? Did he really believe in the message or was it a way to line his own pockets with an empowering phrase that looked good on t-shirts and coffee mugs?

Based on what I knew about Jay before meeting him and based on my initial interactions with him, I found him likeable and passionate. His *Think Big to Win Big* slogan may have sounded a little corny to skeptics like me, but I thought it was authentic. He seemed to believe it.

Regardless of how much Jay Porter believed in the message he was promoting—although I still wasn't *certain* if he did or if he was merely a gifted persuader—the more important question was whether anyone *should* believe it. One could argue the message was not only hokey, but it was irresponsible.

Surely the secret to getting ahead in life wasn't to simply *think bigger*. Based on my personal experience over the last few years, I found such a concept downright offensive.

Was Jay suggesting that the reason I was struggling

so mightily in my career and failing my family was because I wasn't thinking *big* enough? Did he really believe the difference between winners and losers in life was the *size* of one's thinking? And what did a general-sounding phrase such as *think big* even mean? How could you determine if someone was *thinking big* or not?

My goal over the next two weeks was to find answers to those questions.

Contemplating those questions as Jay spoke to his team made me scoff at the whole concept. It made me angry to think Jay was insinuating my bad breaks were due to my small-mindedness. It made me think Ethan had the right idea after all, wanting a story that exposed Jay's *Think Big to Win Big* philosophy for being nothing more than gimmicky, salesman-y, pseudo-motivational nonsense.

The time for pleasantries and quiet observation was over. It was time to start asking Jay some tough questions.

9

The coaching staff worked long into the night on Tuesday, breaking down film and putting together their game plan. I didn't see anything unique about their preparation. All football coaches—from the pros down to the high school level—spent late nights working on these tasks. And all the successful coaches I'd ever been around *loved* doing it.

Most head coaches, especially at the NFL and college levels, tend to be overseers of their programs. That is, their assistants do most of the game planning, skill development, and even play calling. The head coach has final say on those aspects and every other aspect of the program, but the coordinators and their assistants are trusted to do their jobs. The head coach oversees and often overrides decisions, but most don't micromanage every little detail. There aren't enough hours in the day to run a football team that way.

Still, most head coaches can't resist the lure of

spending hours breaking down film—that is, rewatching game footage to analyze your opponents and your own team. They may trust their offensive and defensive coordinators, but they also love the analyzing and strategizing. The schemes and strategies are a big part of what drew them to coaching football in the first place.

In this way, Jay was like most other head coaches I'd been around. Every time I popped into his office throughout my first day at the team's facility, I found him quietly analyzing game footage and adding to his book of notes. I had a lot of questions I wanted to ask, but I didn't want to interrupt his workflow.

Around midnight, I decided to call it a night. I had reached a point where continuing to watch coaches analyze film wasn't going to add anything more to the feature I would be writing.

I knocked on Jay's door to tell him I was leaving.

"Heading out already?" he said with a chuckle. "I suppose this stuff gets a little boring to watch from afar."

"It looks fun," I said. "You guys clearly have a passion for what you're doing."

"I can't imagine doing anything else."

"How much longer will you be doing this tonight?"

"Honestly, it's time for me to wrap it up. If I don't force myself to stop, I could do it all night. You got anything else for me?"

"Actually, yes, I have some questions, but they can wait until tomorrow. I don't want to take away from your prep work."

"Now is as good a time as any," Jay said, rubbing his eyes. "I could use a change of scenery. You hungry?"

I checked my watch. "It's after midnight."

Jay laughed. "I'm a night owl and I forgot to eat dinner."

He led me to the team training table, which was basically a large cafeteria designed to feed the St. Louis Stallions. Like most everything else on this campus, the place was clean and new. At this hour, it was also empty. The kitchen staff had gone home, but Jay had his late-night snacking routine down. I sat at a table as Jay went back to the kitchen and found what he needed in the fridges and pantries. He reemerged with a giant hoagie sandwich and chips on his tray.

"You sure you don't want anything?" he said as he took a seat across from me.

"I'm good," I said, though the sandwich did look delicious.

Jay took a bite, cleared his throat, and said, "So what's your next question?"

"I'd like to know more about your philosophy. The whole 'Think Big to Win Big' thing."

Jay took another bite and smiled. "Not real subtle, is it?" He motioned with his chin to the wall of the cafeteria, where—sure enough—the words *THINK BIG TO WIN BIG* were boldly displayed in blue letters over a silver stripe painted on the wall.

"When did you come up with it?"

"Believe it or not, I started saying that about thirty years ago. After three years of failing to earn a roster spot in the NFL, I figured it was time to put my football days behind me. I got a good job at a huge engineering firm in Houston. It paid well and the future was bright. Only problem was I didn't like my job. I had a bad attitude about it. The job wasn't the problem; it was me. I was so bitter after not making it as a pro football player.

"My boss tried to help me. Instead of firing me, he gave me a handful of books to read. Motivational, self-help type of stuff. They sat in the corner of my apartment for weeks before I finally started thumbing through them. To my surprise, they lit a fire in me. They made me start thinking about what I really wanted to do with my life. I kept thinking about football. I loved the game and missed it like hell. If I couldn't be a player, maybe I could be a coach.

"One night, I was reading a book called, *The Magic of Thinking Big*, and it spoke to me. The main message was: **the bigger you believe, the bigger you will achieve**. The author basically said, **the only thing that separates big-time achievers from everyone else is the size of their thinking, their attitude. Doesn't matter what profession you're in. The biggest achievers are the biggest thinkers.** He said, **you limit yourself by thinking small. The way you choose to think determines how far you'll go in life. And it's your choice. You have control of how you choose to think.**

"Let me tell you, I needed to hear an empowering message like that. I looked at what I was doing with my life and I thought to myself, 'It's time to make some changes. It's time to start thinking bigger.'

"I started devouring these motivational books and they brought me out of my post-football funk. They reminded me what my high school coach had taught me: I could achieve virtually anything if I put my mind to it, kept a good attitude, and put in maximum effort. If someone else could achieve something, so could I. If I started thinking bigger, I'd start achieving bigger.

"I had been questioning beliefs like that after not making it to the NFL, which had been my dream. But I decided it wasn't worth stewing about what didn't work out and it was time to start thinking about what I wanted next. I decided to put the message in those books to the test. What did I have to lose?

"I quit my job and got an assistant coaching job at a small-town junior college, one of those jobs where 'the pay' was basically meals at the school cafeteria and access to a cinder-block dorm room you could sleep in. And you know what? I was in heaven. I was living my purpose.

"There were times when I'd get frustrated, of course. I didn't get along great with the head coach, we had a couple disgruntled players under my watch, and the team facilities were a joke. But anytime I got down, I would tell myself, 'Think Big to Win Big.' It was my little reminder that all I could control was my attitude and if I thought better, things would get better.

"The next year I landed a job as running backs coach at a Division Two college. The pay wasn't a whole lot better, but at least I could afford my own little trailer now, even if it didn't have any air conditioning."

Jay laughed as he remembered his early days of coaching, then took a bite of his sandwich before continuing.

"It can be a tough grind coaching at a small college," he said. "I was there for two years, working for almost nothing, and sleeping in my car on recruiting trips. I was now married and wondering how much longer my new wife would put up with living this way. But I kept reminding myself, 'You've got to think big to win big. Your results will follow your attitude.'

"I constantly fed my mind positive messages. I clarified my goals and the expectations I had for myself. My dream was to be a head coach, and I thought, 'Why not make that happen sooner than later? Plenty of others had done it, why not me?'

"I applied the same questions to the team I was

coaching. We were a losing team at the time, but we had just as much talent as a lot of the other teams in our conference. Why couldn't we start winning right now? Why not us?

"I started reinforcing that mind-body connection to our players. 'If you think big, you'll play big. If you think big, you'll achieve big.' I wanted them to realize **success starts in your mind. How you think determines how you perform and what you can achieve**.

"'Think big to win big.' I would repeat that to myself all through the day sometimes. I would say it to the players I was coaching, teaching them how **your life will follow the way you think. If you see yourself as a big achiever, you'll start achieving big**. I told them we were thinking too small and it was time to start thinking big. **Life will meet you at your level of thinking, so you might as well think big**.

"Well, that message became kind of a rallying cry for our team. Not everyone bought in at first, but it started to catch on with the running backs I was coaching, then spread to the o-linemen, and then to the other offensive players. Next thing you know, the whole team was saying, 'Think big, win big' before practices and games. That attitude permeated the whole program.

"We ended up having a winning season my second year there and I was promoted to offensive coordinator the next season. Two years after that, I got my first Division One job as the running backs coach at Wisconsin State. My living conditions improved a lot that year. And I could finally afford meals like this."

Jay took another bite of his sandwich, finishing it off.

"And the rest is history," I said. "You climbed your way up the college ranks. Eventually got your first head coaching job at North Texas. Then it was Mizzou, where you turned that program into a national power. Two years ago, the St. Louis Stallions shocked the football world by hiring a college coach who had zero NFL experience. And it would appear you've proved all the doubters wrong by winning the NFC Championship in your second season on the job. You're going to sit here and tell me all your success was because you changed your attitude after reading a book about thinking big?"

"It was more than one single book that taught me

that, but yes, when I changed my thinking, everything around me changed with it."

"And you think any average Joe can climb to the top of his profession if he simply thinks big enough, huh? Like you did?"

Jay wiped his mouth with a napkin, crunched up the napkin with his powerful fist, and narrowed his eyes at me. He had picked up on my skepticism loud and clear.

Had I crossed a line?

10

A smile slowly formed on Jay's face.

"You think I'm full of it, don't you?" he said.

"I think you've done an amazing job as a coach," I said. "I think you've cultivated an empowering, easy-to-remember message that your players have bought into. That's not easy to do. I give you credit for your ability to get them on board with your message. But I also think a lot more went into your success than just thinking bigger than your competitors. I think your *Think Big to Win Big* concept is rather vague. I think some people might think your message is more about marketing your own brand than about what works in the real world. And frankly, I think some people could find your message offensive."

"When you say, 'some people,' do you mean people … like *you*?"

I cracked a smile of my own. "As a journalist, it's my job to ask questions. What I personally think is irrelevant."

"Fair enough," Jay said. "What questions do you have for me?"

"Let's start with defining what you mean by thinking *big*. What, *exactly*, does that mean? How does one measure the *size* of their thinking?"

"**To think big means to set big goals and to have big expectations for yourself.** It means having big goals and expectations for your team, your business, your family, whatever group you're a part of.

"**Big thinkers set big goals. They figure, if they're going to go after a goal, they might as well make it a big one. Big thinkers know that it often takes just as much work to achieve a big goal as it does a small goal, so they might as well go after a *big* goal.**"

"Is that really true?" I said. "It seems to me that it would take quite a bit more effort to, say, build a large building than it would a small building."

"Not as much as you might think. Either way, I'm going to have to get financing and hire competent workers to build my building, whether it's big or small. The hard part is convincing the financers to lend me the money and finding the right workers. But once I've figured out how to do that—learning the ins and outs of financing, learning how to find the best workers, electricians, plumbers, and so on—then I can simply repeat the process on a larger scale. I might have to build my way up. Start with a small building, prove myself, and then move to larger building, but the goal should always be to scale up, to keep thinking bigger. If I have to figure out how to do those things anyway—put in all that effort and take all the risks involved with building in the first place—I might as well do it on a bigger scale. That's what it means to think big."

"But what if you're doing all the work yourself, not hiring others? Obviously, it would take a lot more work to build a twenty-story building than it would a one-story shack."

"Doing it all by myself would be a classic example of thinking too small. **We can achieve a lot more as a team than I can as an individual.**"

"Touché," I said with a grin. "But does this theory translate to building a football program?"

"Absolutely," he said. "As a football team, we're all going to be out there busting our butts to prepare for the season. We're lifting, scouting, conditioning. The coaches are analyzing film and putting together game plans. This is the work that must be done. If you're going to be putting in all that work, you might as well be thinking big about what you want to ultimately accomplish. That means setting big goals, having big expectations for yourself and your team. Seeing yourself as a big achiever. It all starts in your mind.

"Here's the thing to remember. Every other team is preparing for games very similar to the way we are. Every team worth a damn is crushing it in the weight room, studying film, doing their homework to be mentally prepared. Every coaching staff is spending endless hours scouting their opponents and putting together innovative strategies to help them win. **Every team knows** *what* **to do to get physically and mentally prepared for an opponent.** *How* **they do it week in and week out is the difference maker. How well you do something is determined by your attitude. No matter your profession, your attitude can be a crucial competitive advantage for you. Thinking big is an attitude that gives you a competitive advantage over those that choose to think small."**

I shook my head. "Are you implying the key to winning a championship is simply setting a goal to win a championship?"

"That's a big part of it," Jay said. "**To be a championship team, you have to build a championship culture. Your team's culture is determined by your team's attitude.** Like the great basketball coach Pat Riley said, 'To be a championship team, you have to think championship thoughts.'

"Now, everyone has to believe they can do it and that type of buy-in takes time. You can't walk into the locker room of a team that hasn't had a winning season in decades and tell them on day one we're going to win it all this year. Nobody will buy into that message because losing has been a way of life, it's a part of the culture. Winning it all is a goal that feels too far away.

"But a new coach can and must help his team think bigger on day one. That might mean setting a goal to finish above five hundred or becoming the most improved team in your conference, but a leader must start changing the culture on day one. **How do you change the culture? By changing the way you think. Changing the expectations.**

"Experience has taught me it takes time to convince a losing program that thinking different will lead to different results. But once they start achieving small results—even something like hitting new records in the weight room—they'll start believing in the message, building on what they're achieving. They'll start asking themselves, 'If changing my attitude helped me achieve that, then why not this?'

"That's where expectations come in. I don't know exactly why or how it works, but **life has taught me that what I *expect* to happen has a huge influence on what actually ends up happening**.

"If I expect more of myself, I achieve more. If I expect to be a winner, I'm more likely to win. If I expect to achieve a specific goal, I'm much more likely to achieve that goal.

"**Whether we realize it or not, we're living up to—or down to—the expectations we set for ourselves. Life tends to give us what we think we deserve; what we think we're worthy of.**

"Most people set their expectations way too low. They think by playing it safe, they're saving themselves from disappointment. They think, 'If I set low expectations for myself, I know I can meet those expectations and I won't get frustrated by falling short.' Or, usually because they've been taught this by someone else, they think they don't deserve to see their dreams come true. They think they're unworthy of success on a big level. That's how small thinkers think.

"**Big thinkers have big expectations. They know that by setting big expectations, their mind will work to fulfill those expectations.** This often happens on a subconscious level. You notice things you wouldn't otherwise notice. You try things you wouldn't have otherwise tried. **Your mind does everything it can to reach the expectations you have set for yourself.** It's amazing how good the mind is at reaching those expectations. Sometimes the results are damn-near miraculous.

"**You achieve a lot more when you *expect* yourself to achieve a lot more. You find a way. Simple as that.**"

"But it's *not* that simple," I said, growing irritated by what I was hearing. "I'm the perfect example. I moved out to L.A. with big goals and big expectations for myself. I was hired as a high school beat writer and my plan was to work my way up to sports columnist and write bestselling books. Those things didn't happen for me. The paper I worked for went under and no publisher was interested in my book ideas. Three years have gone by and I'm *still* searching for a fulltime writing job."

Jay adjusted his cap and gave me a concerned look. "I hear ya, man, life has a way of knocking us off track."

"No, that's not what you said before." I raised my voice. I was revealing more of my personal views than I planned, more than I even realized I was harboring. "You said the key to life was thinking big. According to you, if we set big goals and have big expectations, we'll reach those goals and fulfil those expectations. But that didn't happen for me. Your whole message implies that life's losers are where they are because they're not thinking big enough. It doesn't take into account people's varying circumstances and the bad breaks that so often happen. If you ask me, that's why your message is so disingenuous and, frankly, *offensive* to some people."

"And I assume you'd include yourself in that group of 'some people' who find my message offensive, am I right?"

I shrugged. "I suppose so."

Jay leaned back, still showing empathy in his eyes.

"Good, I want you to be honest with me. My life changed when I started being honest with myself."

11

Jay spent the next few minutes telling me about his initial years after college. How he tried out for three different NFL squads, but never made the team. He told me about his two seasons in the Canadian Football League and then being cut from the team prior to his third year there.

"I didn't know what to do with my life," he said. "I thought I was born to be a football player. My career wasn't supposed to end when I was twenty-five, without playing a single snap in the NFL. I guess you could say, I fell short of my expectations."

"See," I said, with a little more glee in my voice than I should've had. "You were thinking big, you were expecting big, but it didn't work out for you. That goes against your whole philosophy."

"At the time, I hadn't fully developed my philosophy. I was a young guy who desperately wanted to be a pro football player, but wanting something badly enough doesn't always make it happen.

"Years ago, I heard Barry Switzer speak at a coaches' conference. He's the legendary coach who won three national titles in college and a Super Bowl in the NFL. He said, 'The game is ninety percent mental. The other ten percent is being six-foot-four, two hundred and forty pounds, and running a four-four forty.'"

Jay and I both laughed.

"You're making *my* point," I said. "You can set big goals and think as big as you want, but it won't make a difference if you don't have the talent or genetics to achieve whatever it is you're trying to achieve."

"That's where you're wrong," Jay said. "It will make a huge difference. **A think-big attitude won't make it so you can do *anything*, but it will make it so you can do *everything* better. It will make it so you can climb much higher than if you were thinking small.** It was Zig Ziglar who said something along those lines.

"After I faced the reality that I couldn't make it as a player in the NFL, I told you how I got pretty bitter and cynical. I felt like the world owed me my dream and when it didn't come true, I thought, 'What's the point of dreaming?' I had aimed high. I had gone after my dream expecting it to come true, but it didn't. I thought all that big dreaming was a waste because I didn't achieve what I set out to achieve.

"Only later did I realize I was looking at it all wrong. No, I didn't make it to the NFL as a player. But I did earn a scholarship as a walk-on at Texas A&M. I did become a starter who made all-conference. I did play two years of professional football in Canada. I did at least get invited to training camp with three different NFL teams.

"Why didn't I make a roster? Probably because I wasn't six-four, two-forty, and I most definitely couldn't run a four-four forty. I didn't have the size, speed, and talent to make an NFL roster. That's the bottom line.

"But most people told me I didn't have the size, speed, or talent to make the roster of one of the top college football teams in the nation. They said I was wasting my time walking on. They certainly didn't think I would ever earn a scholarship and a starting position. They didn't think I'd eventually play pro football.

"You're right. I didn't have the talent to make it as a player in the NFL, but I took the talent I did have and went a lot further than anyone else thought I could. I can look back and say that I got the most I could possibly get out of the talent I did have. And I did that because I aimed high, I had huge expectations for myself, and I worked my butt off to maximize what I had.

"That's what winning is to me. **Winning means getting the most you possibly can out of what you've got. To get the most you can out of what you've got, you have to enlarge your vision and think as big as you possibly can.** Think big to win big.

"It was working at a job I didn't like and reading those motivational books I told you about that made me realize my optimistic attitude as a player hadn't *let me down*. It had fueled me to be the best I could be, which was a helluva lot more than anyone thought I could be.

"Me, a kid from a middle-of-nowhere town in Texas, who only started one year on his high school team, ended up playing *pro* football. I might not have ended up exactly where I aimed, but I came awful close and ended up a lot higher than I would have if I had not had such big expectations for myself.

"Here's *my* point, Sean. **Can I promise that if you think big, you'll accomplish every single thing you set out to do? No. That's not reality.** I never made it onto an NFL roster and I never won a national title when I was coaching at Mizzou. **But, thinking big will take you way further than you could possibly go by thinking small. It will get you as close to your maximum potential as possible, which is how I define** *winning*."

"And here you are, in the NFL now," I said, "but as a coach."

Jay gave several quick nods. "I think about that a lot. I never stopped aiming for the NFL. It didn't happen the way I wanted it to as a twenty-two-year-old kid, but it did happen. Eventually, I made it here.

"And, well, this sounds cheesy, but … ah, never mind."

Jay's eyes misted up and he adjusted his cap. He stood up abruptly, checking his watch.

"No, what?" I said. "Please finish."

"I think about my wife and my kids," he said. "Had my dream of playing in the NFL happened, I would not have met my wife at that small college I'd never heard of before I coached there."

Jay paused to gather himself. Then continued.

"I tell our players to think big, but trust in a higher power. God knows things we don't know, and sometimes the dream we have isn't meant to be because a bigger and better dream is intended for us. **Think big, aim for your highest goals, but always keep in mind that a greater plan than you can perceive may be unfolding.**"

I was quiet for a moment, reflecting on what Jay had said. He had given his philosophy a lot more thought than I realized. It was more than bumper-sticker motivation.

"And with that, why don't we call it a night," Jay said. "We can pick up on this stuff tomorrow. I love talking about it. Helps me clarify why I believe in it so strongly."

12

I was exhausted when I got back at my hotel room, but I had trouble falling asleep. As I looked over my notes and replayed my conversations with Jay, a few of his statements kept racing through my mind.

Success starts in your mind.

The only thing that separates big-time achievers from everyone else is the size of their thinking, their attitude.

Your life will follow the way you think. And it's your choice. You get to choose how you think.

Life has taught me that what I expect to happen has a huge influence on what actually ends up happening.

Life tends to give us what we think we deserve; what we think we're worthy of.

You limit yourself by thinking small.

I tossed and turned.

Was I limiting myself with my thinking? Had I let bitterness and cynicism overtake me after losing my job, the same way Jay had struggled after his dreams of playing in the NFL ended? Had I created a string of bad breaks with my own petty, negative thinking? Was I aiming too low? Had I lowered my expectations about what I was capable of? Why had I given up on writing books? Had I given up on my big dreams too quickly? Had I prematurely convinced myself that such dreams were no longer attainable?

Okay, I reasoned with myself, *in the aftermath of losing my job, I did lower my expectations. But wasn't that the practical thing to do?*

Whether it was practical or not, I had to admit I spent an awful lot of time complaining to anyone who would listen about how journalism was dying, how there were no jobs available, and how nobody wanted to read books anymore. I complained about the cost of living in L.A., my student loan debt, and how my degree was worthless.

Was all that complaining conditioning me to expect the negative? To see myself as a failure? Was I expecting to fail? Was I living *down* to my own expectations?

Would my life be different right now if I had adopted Jay's *Think Big to Win Big* attitude three years ago? Could it be drastically different if I chose to adopt that philosophy right now?

I finally drifted to sleep wondering if maybe—just maybe—I wasn't the victim I had conditioned myself to believe I was. Maybe I was more responsible for my failures than I wanted to admit. And if I had helped create the difficult condition I was living through, maybe Jay was right and I had the power to *change* my condition by changing my thinking.

It was an exciting thought.

13

I watched the Stallions' Wednesday afternoon practice at the team's indoor facility. It had been several years since I last stood on the sidelines at an NFL practice or game. The size of these guys, their speed and quickness, their athleticism, the timing and precision with which they executed their plays—it was impressive to watch from this vantage point. There was no denying what an elite level these men were performing at.

I was also impressed by how quickly the players could take the intensity from zero to 100. There was hip hop music playing on the loud speakers and the players were keeping it loose and joking with one another between drills. But as soon as the drill or play began, I saw intense collisions, guys fighting with everything they had.

Several times during practice, Jay or one of the other coaches or players would yell out, "Think big," and other nearby players would respond with, "Win big!"

Jay told me he wanted the message hammered into his players' psyche. He wanted the connection between what you thought and how you performed to be seamlessly integrated into each player's thought process. He wanted it repeated in their minds so often that they subconsciously accepted it.

"**Thoughts determine actions**," he told me. "**Once you realize that, you learn to take your thoughts seriously. You recognize negative self-talk and realize you better change those thoughts to something positive if you want your actions and results to be positive.**"

Another phrase I heard repeated often that afternoon was, "Six seconds." A coach sometimes said it before the start of a play and players nodded. Players sometimes said it to each other before adding an encouraging fist bump or tap on the helmet.

Later that night, hours after practice had ended, I was hanging around the offices and Jay told me he needed to get outside for some fresh air. I grabbed my coat and my tape recorder and joined him for a stroll around the campus, which was lit up by plenty of lights overhead. It was the perfect, low-key way to resume our conversation.

"Six seconds," I said. "I heard that multiple times at practice today. What's that all about?"

"Six seconds is the length of an average play in football," Jay said, fog rolling from his mouth as he spoke on this cold St. Louis night. "Four to six seconds, to be exact, but the point is to remind our players constantly that we're asking for six seconds of all-out effort and intensity. You might be tired, you might be drained, you might have other things fighting for your headspace, but for the next six seconds we need to be locked in, focused, and enthusiastic. Anybody can give their all for six seconds.

"It's also a reminder to compartmentalize goals. We're always talking about thinking big. That means having big team goals and dreams. But big goals are achieved in small increments. To be specific, games are won in six-second increments. You have to break all your goals down to smaller objectives. Otherwise, you'll overwhelm yourself."

"How so?" I said, a little winded as I kept up with Jay's pace around the outdoor practice field.

"Like we talked about yesterday, it's important to have big goals and long-term expectations for yourself. That's what keeps you excited. Things like winning your division, winning a Super Bowl, getting into the Hall of Fame, that sort of stuff. That's what thinking big is all about.

"But, a lot of those things are so far out and involve so many things you don't specifically control that you can loose sight of what you're supposed to do in this very moment.

"**Big thinkers know that big goals are only accomplished through small, incremental, and *consistent* actions.** In our case, that means one rep, one play, one six-second increment at a time. You don't win a game by worrying about what the score will be sixty minutes from now. **You win a game one play at a time, with all your focus on your effort and attitude during that one single play. That's all you can control.**

"I want guys to set big expectations for themselves and visualize holding up the Lombardi Trophy at the end of the season. That type of excitement drives you and when you visualize something like that it makes it much more likely you'll experience it—many studies have proven that. But you have to remember those big expectations you've set for yourself are only achieved one moment at a time.

"You can't win this week's game if you're worrying about last week's loss or thinking about who you're playing two or three weeks from now. You have to focus on the task at hand. You have to break down your goal into smaller and smaller objectives until your only focus in the heat of battle is on what you have to do in the next moment. Championships are won one week at a time, one day at a time, one practice at a time, one rep at a time, one play at a time, one six-second battle at a time."

"I think I get it," I said with a smile.

"Six seconds is the reminder to focus only on the present moment. Think big, but focus on the six seconds in front of you. **Think about your big goals and envision your dreams coming true, especially at night or in the morning. Those visions will drive you. But when it's time to go to work, you have to focus only on the task at hand.**

"That's how winning at anything is accomplished. You're a writer; it's the same for you. When you talk about writing books and articles, you know those things are accomplished one page at a time. I imagine if you got so focused on what the end product has to look like or what your editor might think of it, it would overwhelm you to the point you would freeze up with doubt and you wouldn't be able to achieve the task at hand: the page, the paragraph, the sentence. Am I right?"

I chuckled. "More than you know."

"Consistency is the key," Jay said. "**Big goals are only achieved with small, *consistent* action. Small thinkers don't get this. They're always looking for shortcuts. They're looking for ways to avoid the consistent, incremental action required to get you to your big goals.** When they don't get there as fast as they hoped, they get frustrated. They lower their goals or quit altogether.

"Big thinkers know that big, long-term results only come from consistent, short-term habits and actions. **You have to keep stacking those smaller achievements on top of one another. Eventually, you'll reach the top.**

"Coaching college, I used to tell my teams before the season, 'Aim for twelve-and-oh, but focus on one-and-oh.' My point was that 'the guy at the top of the mountain didn't fall there.' That's a Lombardi quote. You work your way to the top one step at a time. Nobody wakes up one morning and discovers they're twelve-and-oh, undefeated champs. It happens one game at a time. One practice at a time, one rep at a time—"

"—Six seconds at a time," I said.

"You got it. And not only does focusing on the moment protect you from being overwhelmed by your long-term goals, but it also keeps you focused in times of adversity. Football is a tough sport. Like life, you're going to make mistakes and you're going to get knocked down. But whenever something bad happens, you have to immediately remind yourself what's done is done and it's the *next* six seconds that matter now.

"**If there's one thing I've learned about life, it's that those who rebound fastest from adversity end up winning most often.** Keeping that six-second mentality helps you do that. It reminds you no matter how bad things are or how frustrated you are with what has happened, you can choose to enjoy the *next* task, the *next* six seconds of battle.

"**The key is to keep moving forward. Regardless**

of what happened in the past, focus on what you can do *now.*

"It's all about taking that next step in front of you. When you get blindsided by adversity, it's easy to overreact and think, 'Now I'll never reach my goal, now I'll never get back on track.' Having a big vision can feel so far away when something just knocked you off course.

"**In those moments of adversity, you must take control of your self-talk. Drown out that negative voice by saying to yourself, 'Focus on the next step and the next step only.' Ask yourself, 'What can I do *right this moment* that will get me just a small step closer to my goal?' That's how you get back on track.** That's why we're constantly reminding each other to focus on six seconds at a time.

"It's all about taking the *next* step. Huge goals are achieved one small step at a time. Championships are won six seconds at a time."

"That's good stuff," I said. "Not to get too personal, but that's something I've struggled with. I was blindsided when the paper I worked for closed up shop. I felt like all the big plans I had for my career fell apart. I couldn't stop ruminating about what happened. How I should have seen it coming sooner, how it was so unfair, how I shouldn't have taken the job in the first place, how I was so stupid for chasing this career. Took me to a dark place of bitterness and self-pity. I'm not sure I ever climbed out of it."

Jay stopped and gave me an empathetic nod. "We've all been there."

I was suddenly self-conscious. I had shared too much with a guy I barely knew, a guy who had a lot bigger things to worry about at the moment than the three-year pity party some random reporter had been throwing for himself. This was unprofessional of me.

I forced a laugh. "Sorry, Jay. That's probably a lot more than you wanted to know about me."

"Don't be sorry. I wish more people would open up about the things they're dealing with. *Everybody's* dealing with something, and we would all be a lot wiser if we talked openly about it and learned from each other."

I nodded, but kept my eyes low. "I appreciate it."

"Let's head back inside." Jay gave me a slap on the shoulder. "I think I might have a way of looking at things that can help you."

14

Jay led me to his office. He walked behind his desk, grabbed a picture frame, and flipped it around to reveal the front.

It wasn't a picture. It was a simple plaque, which read: YOU ARE BIGGER THAN YOUR PROBLEMS.

"I was once an assistant coach when our entire staff got fired," Jay said. "The A.D. wanted to make a change and a new head coach brought in his own staff. We all got the boot. I know it's part of the profession, but the timing is never good when it happens. I was in my early thirties, we just had our second kid, bought our first house, all that.

"I was devastated. My career had been on the rise. I was on a Big Ten staff at Illinois and halfway into the season we were four-and-two with rumors that our offensive coordinator would soon be offered a head job somewhere. My head coach told me if he left, I'd be the front-runner to replace him. I was on cloud nine. Then our starting quarterback goes down, so does our top receiver, and six weeks later, the season is over and we're five-and-seven. We all get fired.

"It happened so fast, none of us were prepared. I'm clearing out my stuff and calling every coach I know that might be hiring. I'm freaking out. The hiring season doesn't last long and you don't want to miss your window.

"Well, as I'm clearing out my office, one of the older coaches on our staff, Marvin Campbell, is walking around whistling, smiling, cracking jokes. I ask him, 'Did you already get on another staff?'

"'Not yet,' he says. 'But I'm sure I will.'

"I tell him, 'I wish I was as sure as you. I just bought a house, just had a kid, I've got no leads.' On and on I go, complaining and telling him about all the problems I have.

"Marv, who is about twenty years older than me, turns to me and says, 'Don't worry about it. Stressing about it isn't going to help you one bit. Aren't you the one always saying to think big? You need to remind yourself, *you are bigger than your problems*. A setback like this isn't gonna keep you down. It sure as hell isn't gonna keep me down.'

"Man, did I need those words at that moment. It reminded me that I had a choice. I could choose my attitude even in an extremely difficult moment. I couldn't do anything about being fired, but I could choose to respond with an optimistic attitude, like Marv was doing.

"**It's easy to preach thinking big and staying positive when things are going well. It's when you get blindsided by adversity that you have to dig deep and tell yourself,** *I am bigger than my problems.*

"**Saying those words—***I am bigger than my problems***—lifts you up inside.** It's a reminder that you have the power to overcome whatever problem you are facing. You might not be in control of what happened, but you are in control of your attitude and what you do next. That's empowering.

"When things go wrong, you can choose to have a bad attitude—complaining, whining, worrying—or you can choose to have a positive attitude—attacking, adapting, and *deciding* to find a way forward and be enthusiastic no matter what.

"**Most problems can be solved by choosing to think bigger.** That means you stop asking questions like, 'Why me?' or 'How will I ever survive this?' And instead ask yourself questions like, 'How can I think bigger about this? What possibilities are opening up for me because of this problem? How can I turn this negative into a positive? How could this problem actually end up being a good thing for me?' That type of thinking forces your mind to focus on positive solutions.

"**It's your choice. You can choose to see your problem as an insurmountable obstacle, or you can choose to see *yourself* as bigger than your problem.**"

"That's easier said than done," I said, now sitting in Jay's office with my tape recorder running.

"Isn't everything?" he said. "Sure, it's easy to worry and stress out. It's easy to throw yourself a pity party and let everyone tell you how sorry they are for you. That's human nature, our default reaction to problems. But where does that get you?

"It's hard to stay positive and enthusiastic when it feels like everything is going wrong. It's hard to keep telling yourself you'll find a way forward when you get hit with obstacle after obstacle. It's hard to attack and adapt when you liked the way things were going and you wish you *didn't* have to adapt. But **only a positive, attack-and-adapt attitude will get you from**

where you are to where you want to be.

"That's what it means to think big. Big thinkers are always excited about the future. They focus on all the things they want to accomplish. When problems come up and knock them off course, they adopt a find-a-way-forward mentality. They tell themselves they are bigger than the problem. They may be down, but they will not stay down. They are too big to stay down. **Big thinkers always believe they are *destined* for greatness**.

"Losses are going to happen. I've never met a coach who retired undefeated. *Think Big to Win Big* doesn't mean if you think big enough and positive enough, you'll never lose a game. That's not reality. But here's the key. **You have to *decide* how you're going to respond to failure and defeat. Big thinkers see themselves as bigger than the problem. Small thinkers see the problem as too big for them. Big thinkers see every problem as temporary. Small thinkers see every problem as permanent. That's the difference in attitude.**

"**You can lose games, but you haven't been defeated until you quit on your dream. When you choose to see a problem as *permanent*, you're essentially quitting on your dream.**"

I lowered my eyes, thinking about how I had reacted to adversity. I had spent most of the last three years sulking in defeat, making dozens of excuses for why I could no longer achieve the goals I had originally set. I never tried to change the one thing Jay was saying could help me get back on track: *my attitude.*

15

"I hear what you're saying," I said, "but some problems *are* really big. I got fired not because I was doing a poor job, but because my industry was consolidating. I reached out to dozens of nearby papers and couldn't find a single one looking to hire a sportswriter. In my situation, the problem *was* too big for me. There was nothing I could do about it."

"**The expectations you set for yourself have a strong tendency to come about**," Jay said. "I know you don't want to hear that, but that's what I think of when I hear you say, 'There was *nothing* I could do.' There's always something you can do to keep moving forward. And it sounds like you *did* do something, otherwise you wouldn't be here right now, working for *The Cheap Seats*."

"Freelance work," I said. "I've landed stories here and there, but nothing that has led to a regular job. The pay is nowhere near fulltime."

"What about the books you said you wanted to write? You told me that was one of your dreams."

"I've been too busy trying to freelance and working as a driver to make ends meet. I don't have the time to work on books."

"You don't have the time or you don't have the enthusiasm to keep fighting for your dreams?"

I started to reactively defend myself, but no words came out. Jay was right. I wasn't spending sixteen hours a day in my car. I wasn't physically out of time. I was out of passion. I was disgruntled by all I had been through and didn't have the burning desire to chase those dreams anymore.

"Maybe you're right," I finally said. "Maybe I *don't* have the enthusiasm to keep chasing the goals I once had. I'm not twenty-five anymore. I've grown up and faced reality. Right now, I don't need my dream job. I just want a regular, steady writing job. That's all I'm asking for and that's what I'm hoping this story leads to with *The Cheap Seats*. If I get back on track with regular work, get some bills paid off, *then* I can start thinking about bigger dreams again."

"Why wait?" Jay said. "Why not do both? Why not rekindle that fire you had to be a bestselling author and write some books between writing articles? This is a perfect opportunity to be bigger than your problem.

"**Don't wait for all your problems to go away before you chase your dream. If you do that, you'll be waiting forever.** Don't put your goals on hold just because the original path you mapped out took a detour. Attack and adapt. You gotta keep fighting for that original vision you had for yourself. You gotta *expect* your dreams to come true. Don't bury that fire, rekindle it. **Enthusiasm is the fuel for achieving big dreams.** You gotta have it."

"And how exactly does a person force themselves to be enthusiastic when the world has beat them to a pulp? It's hard to be passionate about something when you're stressed about bills and worried you are wasting time chasing unrealistic goals."

"Start by visualizing your biggest dreams coming true. See your name on a bestselling book cover. Imagine what it would feel like to have your dream job as a sports columnist. Don't worry about whether it's supposedly *realistic* or not, just let yourself dream like you did when you first moved out to L.A. with all that ambition.

"**Allowing yourself to visualize your dreams coming true is what generates enthusiasm. And you need to be enthusiastic about a goal if you're going to keep chasing it when times get tough. Big thinkers have big enthusiasm.**

"When I was a young coach, working long hours for next-to-nothing pay, I used to imagine what it would be like to someday be a head coach. I'd think about it on my runs, lying in bed at the end of the day, daydreaming while driving on those long recruiting trips. I imagined all the details. What I would say at my opening press conference, what kind of offense and defense we would run, how I would recruit, who I would hire on my staff, the kind of house I would live in, what our practice schedule would look like, what I would say at speaking engagements and after big wins, what it would feel like to hold up a championship trophy at the end of the season. Every little detail I could think of, I allowed myself to daydream and imagine those things coming true.

"Doing this got me fired up. Whenever I had a bad day or felt like things weren't going well, I could call on those dreams and get my fire back.

"When you think big, you start to feel bigger. When

you think about your biggest dreams coming true, something physically happens. You stand a little taller. You see yourself as a bigger person.

"A lot of people might say I was being childish with my daydreams, irresponsible with my time, or unrealistic about my goals. But you know what? Most of what I visualized ended up coming true. And when I got my opportunity to be a head coach, all that mental preparation paid off. I was focused. I had a clear plan because for years I'd been working out all the details in my mind.

"Allow yourself to dream big. Enjoy those moments of visualizing. The more detailed your visualization, the better prepared you will be and the more likely it will be to come true. Don't feel guilty about it. Don't view it as a waste of time or as something that is irresponsible. It's *essential* to your success.

"Our team goes through visualization exercises every Saturday night before a game. We close our eyes and imagine ourselves succeeding. We visualize making big plays and overcoming obstacles. We train our minds to think big.

"The thing is, **everybody visualizes and dreams**

about the future. Small thinkers spend more time thinking about everything that could go wrong. They visualize negative outcomes, they dwell on past mistakes, and they stress themselves out thinking about all the obstacles in their way. Big thinkers spend more time thinking about everything that could go right. They visualize positive outcomes, they focus on the future they want to experience, and they imagine themselves overcoming any adversity they might encounter.

"I've found that if you don't take an active role in visualizing the future you want, you'll get blasted by negative thoughts and worries. Eventually, all that negativity and cynicism will lead to fear and bitterness. When that happens, you'll lose track of what you really want out of life. You'll quit on your goals.

"Does that sound familiar?"

I nodded. "Unfortunately."

"Passion and enthusiasm will overcome stress and worry," Jay said. "That's why big thinkers are always chasing a *big* passion. But no matter how passionate and enthusiastic you are, problems will come. When that happens, you have to do what you can to solve the problem without letting the problem consume you. No matter how big the problem is, don't let it be *all* you think about. Take some time to step away during a crisis and envision your dream coming true. Don't let a problem overwhelm you to the point that you forget *why* you want to achieve your dream. Thinking about *why* you want it so bad in the first place is how you rekindle your fire.

"Dreaming big about the future is how you create hope. And hope is *essential* to happiness."

Jay was once again forcing me to take a close look at my life and I didn't like what I was seeing.

When was the last time I had been *passionate* about what I was doing and not merely looking to survive another day? It had been too long since I'd allowed myself to dream about being a national sports columnist or writing bestselling books. I was jaded. For the past three years, all I had been focusing on was what a raw deal I'd gotten and how unfair the situation was.

I didn't *want* to dream anymore. I thought it would be an irresponsible use of my time. I thought it would get my hopes up and only make me more depressed. I thought it would make me angry to think about dreams that seemed to be slipping further and further away.

But here was Jay telling me I *needed* to dream if I wanted to get my life back on track.

He was not only giving me permission to dream big again, he was telling me it was essential to my wellbeing.

"You're making me think about things I haven't thought about in years," I said. "I can see why your players respond to your message."

"I'm just sharing the things that have helped me in life," Jay said. "If it hadn't been for guys like Marvin Campbell telling me to be bigger than my problems, who knows where I'd be right now?"

"What ended up happening after you were fired?"

"Oh, Marv was right, I landed a job coaching running backs on Mike Leach's staff at Texas Tech. Talk about a big break. This was right when he was turning the program around with his Air Raid offense. I learned a ton from him. After two years on Leach's staff, I was hired as offensive coordinator at Oklahoma. That led me to my first head coaching job at North Texas. I hired Marv as my defensive coordinator and he stayed with me all the way to Mizzou, until he retired. I still talk with him often.

"Problems will come and go, but things tend to work out in the end when you think big and stay focused on the dreams that matter to you most."

16

I want to clarify that during this leadup to the Super Bowl, Jay Porter wasn't spending countless hours acting as my personal life coach. Most of the time I was in St. Louis, I was sitting in on team meetings and interviewing players when I had the chance.

One of those interviews was with running back Jaylin Mack. Only five-foot-six, Mack was the second-smallest running back in the league. Yet, he had rushed for more than 1,100 yards this season. He was one of the vital pieces in St. Louis' offense. Mack told me Jay changed his life by helping him change the way he thought of himself. I couldn't help but see him as the very personification of Jay's *Think Big to Win Big* philosophy, someone who outperformed his physical stature to achieve at such a high level.

I also conducted quick, casual interviews with staff members during my time in St. Louis. From coordinators to entry-level coaches to office managers and maintenance staff, everyone I talked to only had positive things to say about Jay. Again and again, staff members told me Jay was "genuine," "passionate," and "excited about life."

A few times I asked quietly, with a little smile that said, you can trust me, "Off the record, does the *Think Big to Win Big* schtick get a little old sometimes?"

Nobody took the bait. They insisted the philosophy kept them going, kept them motivated. The closest I got to anything disagreeable was an assistant coach telling me, "At first, I'll admit I was skeptical. But look around you. This stuff works."

By all accounts, Jay walked the walk of his *Think Big to Win Big* philosophy.

Every so often, I'd recognize an opportunity to pepper Jay with random questions about his past, his thoughts on the upcoming game, and his life philosophy. Because Jay was the type of coach who enjoyed discussing topics besides just the Xs and Os of football, and because he was a man who seemed sincerely interested in helping others, he ended up giving me some of the most helpful advice I've ever received in what was beginning to feel like random therapy sessions. They weren't planned and I wasn't asking for them. They just sort of ... happened.

On Thursday, I flew back to Los Angeles. I would be meeting back up with Jay and his team once they arrived in Southern California for Super Bowl week.

During my flight home, I took some time to daydream about the goals I once had. I imagined myself as a bestselling author, like the sportswriters I had grown up reading. That led me to brainstorming several new book ideas, something I hadn't done in three years. They just started popping into my head, one after another. I hastily wrote down my thoughts as soon as they entered my mind, making sure I caught them before they faded away. The passenger next to me must have thought I was nuts as I scribbled in my notebook, grinning from ear to ear.

For the first time in years, I was starting to feel *enthusiastic* about what my future might look like. Thanks to Jay, I was rekindling the fire inside.

17

I spent the weekend listening to recordings of my conversations with Jay and other Stallion coaches and players. I read through and added to my extensive notes as I pieced together how I planned to write the feature on Coach Porter.

It didn't take me long to figure out I had a problem. This story was most definitely *not* going in the direction Ethan wanted it to.

When I accepted this assignment, I intended to take my story in the controversial — or at least, *adversarial* — angle Ethan had asked for. But as I sat at my kitchen table, surrounded by pages of notes, I could no longer see a way to make that angle work without being disingenuous.

From everything I had witnessed during my time in St. Louis, Jay was a brilliant football mind, an extremely hard worker, and an authentic leader. He had the respect and support of every player and coach

I talked to while on the Stallions' campus. Even the team's General Manager told me Jay had personally helped him change his outlook on life.

I could see why. Jay was forcing *me* to confront the issues I was struggling with. He seemed genuinely interested in helping me change my attitude and the trajectory of my life. The guy actually *cared* about a freelance reporter he had never heard of a week ago.

How could I turn around and write a scathing article on him?

Beyond my personal appreciation for what Jay was doing for me, there was also the pesky little fact that I didn't *have* any dirt on him. The negative directions I thought I might be able to take with the article — portraying him as a surprisingly shrewd, self-interested promoter looking to cash in on his once-in-a-lifetime opportunity, or simply as a likeable-but-clownish coach who lucked into the greatest opportunity of his career and was now in over his head — would be untrue. How could I force an angle I knew wasn't truthful?

Sunday afternoon, one week before the Super Bowl, I called Ethan to let him know where I was with the story. I did my best to pitch a new direction for the piece.

"The feature is coming along great," I said. "Jay and his staff have been more helpful than we could have hoped for."

"Great to hear," Ethan said over the phone.

"There is a slight issue, though. Actually, I think it's a golden opportunity."

"Uh oh," he said.

"No really, I think it's a good thing. I followed Porter around for two full days, sitting in on every meeting and interaction with the team. I've talked with several guys on his staff and multiple players. The truth is, they all love the guy."

"Hmm. Of course they're going to say that. Their livelihoods depend on his approval."

"I think it's more than that. I think Porter is the real deal, a legit great leader. The access I'm getting, some of the quotes he's given me, it's outstanding stuff. Nobody else is going to have what I have. I'd like to write the ultimate insider story about a coach who just might shock the world on Sunday. I'm telling you, if he finds a way to win—or even keeps the game close—we're going to have the inside story about why this guy could be the next great NFL coach. With the stuff he's given me, *everyone* will be talking about this story."

Ethan sighed. "You're drinking the Kool-Aid, Sean. I know everyone thinks Porter is a good dude. I do too. But he's been in this league for two seasons. He hasn't paid his dues. There's *no way* he's ready for a moment this big. That's why St. Louis is the biggest underdog in modern Super Bowl history. They don't belong in this game. Everybody knows it.

"I'm not saying you have to trash the guy in your story. But I want you to pull back the curtain and reveal exactly why Porter will be out of his league on Sunday. People are going to read this on Super Bowl morning; I want us to be telling everybody why the game is over before it even begins. How is it gonna look if you write a puff piece about how great Porter is right before they go out and get stomped by three or four touchdowns?"

"What if they win?"

Ethan laughed. "Okay, now I'm *sure* you're drinking the Kool-Aid."

"Ethan, there is something special about this guy. He's more than a catchphrase. I want to show that in my feature. I want to show how he's changing people's lives. I'm telling you, talking with this guy is changing *my* life."

There was a brief moment of silence and I could picture Ethan shaking his head. "Can I be honest with you?"

"Of course," I said.

"You sound like someone who's being manipulated by the subject of his story. It happens all the time in this business. Maybe I picked the wrong guy for the job."

My stomach dropped. "What are you saying?"

"I like you, Sean, I really do. You're a good writer and you've always hit your deadlines with us. I could see you working fulltime for *The Cheap Seats*. But I'm not sure you're ready for this job. You're too afraid of offending people. Readers don't want the news sugarcoated. They want the raw, inside stuff. There's a positive side and a negative side to every story. Fact is, people like reading about the negative more. It's not good or bad, it's just the way it is. Readers want to see *honest* portrayals, flaws and all."

"I'm being as honest as I can. Believe me, I'm the last guy you'd call naive. I pride myself on seeing the world as it is. I would never put a disingenuous spin on a story. But in this case, it would be disingenuous for me *not* to show what a positive impact this coach is having on his team."

"I'm not asking you to be disingenuous. I'm asking you to be professional. Separate your personal feelings and follow the facts."

"That's exactly what I'm doing."

Ethan huffed. He was losing his patience with me. "It sounds like you can't write the story I hired you to write. Let me know now, do I need to find someone who *can* write the story?"

"Ethan, I can't just make up lies."

"Of course not, I would never ask you to do that. But I'd like you to dig deeper. Find some players who will go off the record with you. Every team has disgruntled players. Find them and get them to talk to you. I'm not asking for a hit piece on the guy, but I want to be the one source with the courage to reveal what is really going on behind that good-guy persona, that Cinderella story everyone else will be writing about. That's how we'll drive traffic. That's the type of feature that will get people talking. Trust me, I know what I'm doing."

I wasn't sure how to respond. I understood what

Ethan wanted, but I didn't know if I could give him what he wanted.

"Sean, can you write me this story or do I need to find someone else?"

For a moment, I imagined how Jenny would react if I told her I was walking away from the story. It was the opportunity I had been waiting three years for. She was so thrilled for me when I told her the news. My kids had picked up on our joy and we were all smiling and laughing as I packed my bags for St. Louis a week ago. *Am I really going to tell them I walked away from the feature?* And why exactly *would* I be walking away? Ethan made it clear he wasn't asking me to lie or do anything dishonest. He simply wanted the article to go in a different direction than I wanted. He knew what readers wanted better than I did. Wasn't it my job to do what my boss wanted me to do?

"Sean, you there?"

"I'm here," I said. "I see what you mean and … I can do it. I'm your man for the job."

"Great! Don't let me down. This is a big opportunity for you. *The Cheap Seats* needs to make some noise and if you're the guy who makes that noise for us, there will be a place for you here. I'll make it worth your while. I'm counting on you. Gotta run. Keep me updated and call if you need anything."

18

I spent Sunday evening second-guessing myself.

Was Ethan right? *Was* I approaching this story objectively or had I been blinded by Coach Porter's infectious enthusiasm? Was I seeing only what I wanted to see, focusing on only the good things I saw Jay doing for his team and overlooking the negative consequences of his overly-optimistic philosophy?

I had to admit, I *wanted* Jay and the Stallions to succeed. How could I not? He was a good guy who took the time to show he cared about me. His lessons were forcing me to reevaluate my own thinking and helping me see the world in a new way.

But journalists weren't supposed to have a rooting interest in their subjects. How could I write an unbiased story from that perspective? No wonder Ethan was calling me out.

To be clear, I didn't believe Jay was trying to manipulate me. He wasn't trying to win me over so I would write a nice feature about him. Like most coaches, I don't think he cared much about how he was portrayed in the media. What he cared about was whether he was being the leader he needed to be for his team.

Jay was genuine. I had no doubt about that. He believed strongly in his *Think Big to Win Big* philosophy. He cared about the success of his players and coaches, both on and off the field. From what I could tell, he cared about *my* success. That was who he was. He lived his philosophy and believed it could make a positive difference in *everybody's* life.

I liked Jay and appreciated him. I wanted him to succeed. But that didn't mean I should write a one-sided story on the man.

I told myself that night it was time to start poking holes in Jay's philosophy. It was my job.

Yes, I *really* needed the money and I *really* wanted a fulltime job as a sportswriter. But I wasn't cutting any corners or doing anything immoral, I told myself. This was part of being a journalist. Sometimes you had to be hard on people you liked. It was all about digging deeper and revealing the truth, like Ethan said.

Ethan also said people didn't want to read positive stories. He wanted this article to show what went *wrong* with their season, not what went right. He said people want the negative, the shocking, the damaging news. They don't want stories about how great somebody is; they want stories revealing the flaws behind the person everybody else says is great.

Is that why I hadn't found fulltime work in three years? Was I trying to *sugarcoat* stories, too afraid to offend people, as Ethan said?

I wrestled with my morals the rest of the night. Was it wrong to write a story where you purposely focused on the negative? Was it any worse than writing a story where you focused on the positive because you had a positive bias for the subject?

Ultimately, it came down to this: my boss wanted the story to go in a negative direction. So, if I wanted to stay employed, there was only one option.

It was time to get tougher with Coach Porter and his team.

19

The Monday of Super Bowl week was the traditional Media Day where reporters from all over the nation gathered at podiums set up inside SoFi Stadium to interview players and coaches from both teams. Because it was always such a chaotic day, I knew in advance I would not have any one-on-one time with Jay. I would do my best to compete with hundreds of other reporters to find unique storylines.

When Jay stepped up to the podium, he attracted one of the largest crowds of the day. For nearly an hour, he fielded question after question.

The topics were varied, with questions covering everything from who his childhood heroes were to what his favorite movies were to what his thoughts were on odd-front versus even-front defenses. But the line of questioning that got my attention had to do with Jay's propensity to take big risks.

More than a week after the Stallions' previous

game, reporters still wanted to ask Jay about his decision to go for the win on the final play of regulation in the NFC Championship instead of safely kicking an easy field goal and sending the game into overtime.

"Does last week's decision reveal what you would do if you face a similar situation in the Super Bowl on Sunday?" a reporter asked.

Jay shrugged and smiled. "Probably. At this point, I don't think we're going to surprise anyone with our aggressiveness."

"If you had lost the game on that final play, would you be second-guessing your decision?" Oh, how us sports reporters loved hypothetical questions.

"I'd be second-guessing the play call, our preparation prior to the game, and our execution of the play. I wouldn't be second-guessing the decision to go for the win. You've got to think big to win big. That's who we are. **If you play it too safe, you're going to limit what you achieve in life.**"

That sparked a barrage of follow-up questions. Reporters wanted to know more about what he meant by playing it *too* safe.

"Big thinkers dare to be great," Jay said. "**Small**

thinkers are always thinking about what they can do to avoid risk. Big thinkers are always thinking about what they can do to be great. To be great and win big, you have to be willing to put yourself out there and take some risks. There is no risk-free way to make big dreams happen. Every big achievement requires you to take risks. Those risks may be uncomfortable and scary, but you have to feel the fear and do it anyway. You'll win some and you'll lose some, but to achieve big you've got to be willing to take some chances."

A reporter asked whether he relied on analytics or gut feelings when taking risks and making big decisions.

"Both," Jay said. "You can't be reckless. You have to be prepared and properly analyze the situation. You want to know your odds and you want to know if the risk is worth it. But you ultimately go with your gut, even if it defies the odds. Nobody knows your team like you do. You have to trust your instincts. **Do everything you can to prepare for the situation, then trust your gut.**"

I joined the fray with a follow-up question of my own. "It's human nature to want to alleviate risk. Wouldn't some people say it's irresponsible to take big risks that could have a big downside?"

Jay gave me a half-smile and adjusted his cap before answering.

"I would tell 'some people' they're probably exaggerating the potential downside in their minds. **Failure is temporary. You can always bounce back if you refuse to quit.** I would also say, **if you're waiting for everything to be just right and for all risks to be eliminated before taking a chance and going for something big, you'll be waiting your whole life and never actually going after what you want. You'll be sitting on the sidelines watching others win big**.

"**All big achievements require taking risks. Will some of those risks result in failure? Unfortunately, yes. But big thinkers are okay with that. They get back up and keep on risking. They attack and adapt. They keep moving forward until they hit their target. That's how winning is done.** Sometimes it's two steps forward and one step back, but as long as you're moving forward—some might say, *failing* forward—you'll eventually get to the top of the mountain."

I followed up with, "What would you say to people who are afraid to take such risks?"

"I would say, 'Train you mind to *think big*.' **Big**

thinkers are often accused of being too optimistic. They expect things to work out. And we all know things don't always work out. But big thinkers don't care. They expect to win in the end. They err on the side of thinking *too* big because they know that's way better than aiming too small. Yes, they'll lose some along the way, but they'll keep attacking. They'll learn from each loss, adapt, move forward, and ultimately win big.

"Every great basketball player is convinced he will make the *next* shot regardless of how many shots he's missed. Every great achiever I've studied is convinced his *next* big venture is going to be a huge success no matter if he failed at the previous venture. It's the same in sports, in business, in life. **Big thinkers win big because they're not afraid to get back up, to keep taking risks, and to keep expecting victory. They learn from every mistake and it eventually pays off ... in a very big way."**

I noticed some restless glances from other reporters. We were no longer talking only about football and they knew Jay could talk about this subject all night if we let him. A reporter changed the subject by asking Jay a question about his practice schedule for the week.

When Jay's time at the podium ended, I made my way around to other podiums, listening in and asking questions to players and coaches.

At one point, I noticed Marshall Lewis sitting behind a microphone with a rather small crowd of reporters in front of him. I checked the schedule and confirmed his allotted time with the press had indeed already started. Only a handful of reporters had bothered to show up.

Marshall Lewis was St. Louis' starting quarterback when the season began. Second-year player Troy Wallace had replaced him after a Week Four loss to Atlanta—a week when Marshall had thrown three interceptions and zero touchdowns.

If I was looking for a disgruntled player — or at least someone who might be quietly questioning Jay's brand of think-big optimism — surely it was this guy.

20

When I got to Marshall's media session, I realized one reporter was from Pittsburgh, Pennsylvania, the city Marshall grew up near and played his college ball in. She was cooking up a story for the hometown fans who wanted to know how one of their favorite players was handling his Super Bowl preparation, how ready he was to enter the game if called upon, and what it would mean to win a Super Bowl — starter or not.

The only other reporter I heard asking questions was from one of the national sports networks. His questions weren't quite as feel-good. First, he asked Marshall how he was handling his demotion from starting QB to backup.

"I'm just happy to contribute any way I can to help this team win," Marshall said.

He asked if Marshall felt he should be the starter.

"That's not up to me. All I can say is, if my number gets called, I'll be ready to go."

The reporter asked if Marshall expected to be playing for St. Louis next year or if he would be demanding a trade in the offseason.

Marshall smiled. "I'm not thinking about next season. I'm only focused on where I am right now."

This reporter was looking to drum up controversy, but Marshall didn't take the bait. He answered each question like the eight-year pro that he was.

I listened in, but didn't ask any questions of my own.

The media session was brief, lasting maybe ten minutes. When it was over, Marshall thanked us and stepped away as the few reporters dispersed. I caught up with him before he left the field.

"Marshall, I'm Sean Riley, you might have noticed me last week in St. Louis." I extended my hand and he shook it with a polite nod.

"You handled those questions like a pro," I said. "No distractions from you this week."

"I'm telling the truth."

I raised a skeptical eyebrow. "Of course you are. Listen, I was wondering if I could get some one-on-one time with you. I'm writing a feature about how you guys are preparing for the Super Bowl and everything Jay has done to turn things around. I'm interested to hear what you think of Jay's leadership style, how things have changed since he took over, that sort of thing."

"Coach Porter has done a great job. We're playing in the Super Bowl. What more can I say?"

"You've been in this league for eight years and with St. Louis for four of those years. You've seen the transition like nobody else and I'd love to hear your perspective on how things have changed since Porter arrived. It would help me understand what is going on here. Would you be willing to sit down with me? We could go on or off the record, your call."

"Why would I need to go off the record?" Now it was Marshall's turn to raise a skeptical eyebrow.

"Whatever you're most comfortable with. I want you to be able to speak freely. I've always admired you, how you've carried yourself in this league. Getting traded to an expansion team in the prime of your career, having to carry that team on your shoulders through those rough upstart years, that could not have been easy. You handled it like a Hall of Famer. I'm not sure you get the recognition you deserve for getting the team to where it is right now."

"You're buttering me up," Marshall said with a grin.

"Is it working?"

He laughed. "A little bit."

"You've got such a unique view of how things have turned around. If I could just get half an hour of your time, it would mean so much. What do you say? I won't print anything you're uncomfortable with."

Marshall looked off in the distance, contemplating whether he should play ball with me.

"This feature is going to be a big deal," I said. "I give you my word, you'll be portrayed in a positive light. It will only help your future prospects, whatever those may be."

Marshall gave me a reluctant nod. "Alright. Let's do it."

This was the break I needed for the story. If there was anybody who would love to vent about the inner workings of this team, it had to be the recently benched veteran quarterback. I was about to find out how Jay's leadership style was affecting the entire team. Not just the stars and the starters, but the bench guys, too.

21

Eight seasons ago, Marshall Lewis entered the NFL as Washington's second-round draft pick. He spent his first two seasons in the league as a backup, but became Washington's starter halfway through the third year of his pro career. In Year Four, he led the Commanders to the playoffs. His future looked bright. But then Washington traded him to St. Louis, an expansion franchise in only its second year of existence.

Marshall's first two seasons with St. Louis did not go smoothly. A poor offensive line forced the dual-threat quarterback to spend most of those two seasons running for his life. During that two-year stretch, Marshall missed nine games due to injuries and the Stallions limped their way through back-to-back five-win seasons.

Fans and reporters couldn't deny Marshall's talent, but everyone wondered how long he could hold up with this struggling expansion team. The next year,

Jay Porter was hired as head coach and he drafted quarterback Troy Wallace with his first draft pick. The writing was on the wall: Marshall's days as a Stallion were numbered.

He remained the starter during Jay's first season as head coach. With an improving o-line and defense, the Stallions went 8-9 and Marshall put up the best passing numbers of his NFL career. While fans were anxious to see what Troy Wallace could do under center, no one was surprised to see Marshall Lewis named the starter heading into this season.

After a 1-3 start, however, Jay pulled the trigger and named Wallace the starter for Week Five. Despite some growing pains along the way, Wallace hit his stride in Week Fourteen and the team hadn't lost since. Other than a few drives when Wallace went down with minor injuries, Marshall watched this amazing run to the Super Bowl from the sidelines.

This had to be hard on Marshall. He had weathered the hard times in St. Louis. He had paid the price for three full seasons. Finally, after the most productive season of his career, things started turning around for the franchise … and he got benched.

I was anxious to hear Marshall's version of

everything that happened. There had to be some resentment.

Early Tuesday morning I went to a coffee shop a couple of blocks aways from the hotel where most the Stallions were staying in Los Angeles. Twenty minutes past the time Marshall told me to meet him, I wondered if he had changed his mind about doing the interview.

Deciding against a third cup of coffee, I stood up to leave right when Marshall walked in and gave me a tentative nod. He was wearing sunglasses, a generic Nike hoodie and hat, nothing that would identify him as a St. Louis Stallion.

"I was worried you might be having second thoughts," I said as he took a seat across from me.

"I was. I'm still not sure this is a good idea." He pulled his hat lower, clearly uneasy with his decision to meet me.

I gave him a warm smile, trying to put him at ease. "There is nothing to worry about. I'm not looking to stir up trouble. Seriously, I just want to know what it's like to be you this season. I want to know how this turnaround happened from a wise veteran's perspective."

"I texted Coach Porter before coming here," Marshall said. "I didn't want to do anything behind his back. He said it was fine. He thinks you're a good guy."

Hearing that made me initially feel proud to have won Jay's trust, but then I felt guilty that here I was trying to pry out a disgruntled opinion of him.

I bought Marshall a coffee and spent the next few minutes asking him generic questions about growing up, his time in the NFL, his family—lighthearted things like that. I wanted him to feel comfortable talking with me. Once I could see he was relaxing, I tried to get him to open up about his experiences this season.

"I want to say again how impressed I've been with the way you've handled yourself this year," I said. "You never aired any dirty laundry after you lost the starting job. You said all the right things. But still, as the competitor you are, I imagine this has been hard to go through."

"On the record: I just want to keep doing whatever is best for the team," he said. "I'm here to help us win a Super Bowl by doing whatever they ask me to do. All I want is for us to win. Off the record: watching from the sidelines has been killing me. It's the hardest thing I've ever been through as a football player."

"I can imagine."

"I *knew* something special was about to happen with this team. I could feel it at the end of last season and even more during training camp this year. Things were clicking. The guys were all coming together. We were all on the same page. I knew this was going to be a special season. I really did.

"Even when we started one-and-three and I played terrible against Atlanta, I still thought we were going to be a great team. And I thought *I* was going to be the QB leading us."

"How did you find out you were no longer the starter?"

"Coach Porter called me into his office the Monday after the Atlanta game. He told me man-to-man they were going with Troy. He was honest about it. I could tell he hated having to tell me, but he thought it was best for the team.

"Obviously, it wasn't a total shock. Troy was our number-one draft pick the year before. The fans wanted to see him. But after holding him off during his rookie year and being named the starter at the beginning of this season, I thought this would be my year. I knew I might get traded after the season, but I thought I'd hold on to the starting job this year."

"With the way this season has gone, making it all the way to the Super Bowl, do you think Porter made the right decision?"

"Let me say this, on the record: Troy is the real deal. He's going to be a great quarterback in this league for a very long time. Troy and I are very tight. We're competitors, but we get along great and I want to see him succeed.

"At the same time, I know I still have what it takes to be a starter in this league. I had my best season ever last year, I'm healthier than I've ever been, and I've got several more seasons in me. My best football is yet to come. I believe that and I think my teammates and coaches would tell you the same thing.

"Having said all that—and this needs to be off the record—getting benched was probably the wakeup call I needed. I had to get my mind right. This team was clicking, I could feel it. But did I really think we were a Super-Bowl-caliber team? If I'm being honest, I can't say that. Again, I don't want that printed."

"No problem, but can I ask why you don't want

that printed?"

"I'll talk about it publicly when the time is right. But for now, I know several teams will be interested in trading for me next year and I don't want them thinking I had an attitude problem. I'm just being honest with you. I thought we'd be good. I thought this could be a breakout year for us. But I didn't think we'd go *this* far."

"I don't think many people did," I said with a smile. "Do you think Troy was the difference-maker, then?"

"Talentwise, he and I are very similar QBs. We can both run when we need to. Troy's a bit faster than me, I'll admit that. But I have a stronger arm, he'll tell you that. I think I'm still ahead of him when it comes to reading a defense due to my experience in the league, but he's got that special ability to improvise. Like I said, I think Troy is great. But I think I am, too. I've still got all the tools to win big in this league. I hope that doesn't sound too arrogant, but it's the truth about how I feel.

"Where Troy got the advantage on me was with his mentality. Again, don't print this part. It could really hurt me in the eyes of other teams."

"You have my word," I said.

"I didn't see it at the time I was benched, but I see it now. I had been beaten up pretty good my first two seasons in St. Louis. Last year was a lot better, and you could feel the tide turning for this team. But still, I was a little more cynical than the younger guys about how far we could go. In the offseason, Coach Porter started talking about winning the division and making a Super Bowl run. He kept saying it was time to think bigger, *much* bigger than we had been. The skeptic in me thought we weren't at that level yet. I'd been in this league longer than Porter and most the other guys on our team. I had played against Super Bowl teams. I didn't think we were ready for that level.

"But Troy, he's young and bright-eyed. Like most top draft picks, he was a star in college and hadn't been humbled by this league the way I had been. He showed up full of enthusiasm and he was buying everything Porter was saying. All that *Think Big to Win Big* stuff.

"Don't get me wrong, I liked the message. But looking back, I can see that I wasn't *all in* on it. Not the way Troy and a lot of the other guys were. I had my doubts. And like Coach says, **if you listen to your**

doubts, you will limit what you're capable of.

"So yeah, watching this team from the sidelines has been hard because I want to be out there with them. It's also a reminder to me that I was holding myself and the team back with my attitude. I *wasn't* thinking big enough early in the year. That was the difference between me and Troy. I can admit that now. I see how much I was limiting myself mentally.

"You look at this team now and the results speak for themselves. Once everybody got on board with believing, it's like it unchained our potential. I know we're big underdogs, but I'm telling you, we can win the whole thing. I'm ecstatic for the team. I love these guys."

"So you don't feel any resentment about how everything went down?"

"No. No resentment whatsoever. At first, I was mad. Went down the self-pity path. But after a week or two of watching from the sidelines, I did some self-evaluation and realized I had to take responsibility for where I was. I only had myself to blame."

"And what about Porter specifically? You don't think he maybe pulled the trigger too quickly when he benched you?"

"I've got nothing bad to say about that man. He was honest with me from the start. And after he benched me, he wasn't one of those coaches who acted like I no longer existed. He's always checking in on me, making sure I'm ready to go if called on, telling me how much he believes in me. He knew I was down those first couple of weeks after getting benched, and he took the time to build me back up mentally. He cares about me. I completely trust that man."

So much for getting the backup quarterback to bad-mouth his head coach. If anything, Marshall was giving Jay more praise than you'd expect to hear from the team's superstars.

Though I wasn't getting the controversial quotes that would drive clicks like Ethan wanted, I personally wanted to know more about how Jay won over a veteran like Marshall.

"As a guy who has been in this league awhile," I said, "what was your initial reaction to Porter's philosophy when he arrived in St. Louis? *Think Big to Win Big*. Honestly, what did you think of that?"

"When he first came in with that phrase and we had all these meetings about what it meant, I was skeptical. I thought it sounded a bit over the top—like a college coach trying too hard to fire us up, you know? I wasn't sure how it was going to go over with everyone.

"But the thing is, *he* really believed it. You can tell if someone isn't genuine. Coach Porter is the real deal. He isn't faking it. Seeing how much he believes in his message, you start to buy in. We all did. That enthusiasm becomes contagious the more everyone buys in. It turned the culture around. Made us all start asking, 'Why not us? Why can't *we* make the playoffs? Why can't *we* win the division?'"

"Or even the Super Bowl," I said.

"Exactly. Just took me a little longer to buy into that one.

"If there's one thing I've learned from Coach Porter, it's realizing how much you limit yourself with your thoughts. You have to take responsibility for your attitude. You have to start thinking bigger if you want to start achieving bigger. You have to think big to win big.

"Seeing where this team is now, there's no doubt his message is working. It has changed this team. And it's changed the way I look at my own life.

"I don't know what will happen next for me. I don't

know if I'll get in during the Super Bowl or where I'll be next season. But what I do know is that everything I've been through has prepared me for something really big. I have no doubt about that. I have higher expectations for my future than ever before. *Big* things are coming my way. That, you can print."

22

The Stallions were using a local college facility for their Super Bowl prep and I spent the rest of Tuesday listening in on coach and player meetings. All through the day, I thought about my interview with Marshall. It did not go as I thought it would. Though it didn't give me the clickbait material Ethan wanted me to find, I was personally inspired by the way he handled the adversity he'd experienced this season.

Here was a veteran quarterback who had been through many ups and downs in his career. He had put in his time as a backup. When he got his opportunity as a starter, he engineered an impressive turnaround in Washington. He then suffered through double-digit losses and multiple injuries when he was traded to an overmatched expansion team. He did it all without complaining. Finally, things started clicking for St. Louis and he got his chance to play for a breakout team headed to the Super Bowl. This was every football player's childhood dream—the ultimate goal in this profession. But instead of arriving at this career pinnacle as the starting quarterback, Marshall would be watching the biggest game of his career from the sidelines.

It didn't seem fair. Everything he worked so hard for was happening … but it seemed to be happening to someone else.

At least, that's how it looked to an outsider like me.

Marshall didn't see it that way.

He wasn't resentful. He wasn't wallowing in self-pity, seeing himself as a victim. Instead, he was *growing* from the situation. He was becoming a better man with a better attitude. Instead of whining about the biggest setback of his football career, he was reevaluating himself, owning the mistakes he made, and choosing to think bigger than he ever had before.

Jay was so busy meeting with coaches, analyzing film, and tweaking Super Bowl game plans that I didn't have the chance to interview him. When I got home Tuesday evening, I again agonized over how I was going to take this story in the direction Ethan wanted me to. Marshall was willing to go off the record with me, but even his most honest comments were nothing but supportive of Jay and his leadership style.

On Wednesday, I watched the team practice and noticed how enthusiastic Marshall still was. He carried himself like a confident leader, even if he was QB number two on the depth chart. He fired his passes with precision. He ran through drills like a rookie trying to prove himself on every rep. Several times, I saw him talking with Troy as he pointed at something downfield, teaching the younger quarterback what to look for as he read defensive coverages.

Marshall was a true teammate and impressed me as a confident leader.

The day was so busy I didn't get the chance to ask Jay any one-on-one questions until 11:30 that night. His workday was over and I offered him a ride back to the team hotel, which he accepted.

"I talked with Marshall Lewis yesterday," I said as I drove.

"I heard," Jay said. "He's a great guy and a great player. He'd be starting for most teams in this league."

"I asked him about that."

"I figured that would come up. Marshall believes in himself. He knows he should be a starter."

"But he isn't starting on your team. You benched him. Was that the right decision?"

"Yes. It was the best thing for our team at that moment. But I'll tell you something, it was a really hard call. We've got two outstanding quarterbacks on this roster. That's a good problem to have, but deciding between two great competitors like that isn't easy."

"Any second-guessing?"

"Of course. You've seen our practices; you've seen the way Marshall fires the ball. He's better this year than he was last year. Hell, I think I second-guess the decision every time I see him take a snap. But Troy is also one of the best quarterbacks I've ever been around and he has earned the starting spot for what we want to do. You have to make the best decision you can and move forward."

"Off the record," I said. "With a player as talented as Marshall is, what made the difference in your decision to bench him? Was it his attitude?"

"I've got two great quarterbacks," Jay said. "We're grading them all the time and they are neck and neck. When ability is that close, attitude is always going to be the difference maker."

"You benched Marshall because he had a poor attitude?"

"No. I gave Troy the starting job because he had a better attitude. At that moment in the season, Marshall was down on himself. Most the time, he had a good, positive attitude, but he was starting to doubt himself and he didn't have the enthusiasm we wanted in our field general. He wasn't thinking big enough. And with the talent-level so close between the two, we had to make the change. Yes, attitude made the difference. It *always* makes a difference."

"What's interesting to me is that Marshall doesn't have any resentment about what happened," I said. "Obviously, he wants to be the starter, but he seems to have grown from the situation. He says he realizes now he wasn't thinking big enough and it was holding him back from reaching his potential. Most guys get benched and they tend to sulk and develop a worse attitude. Marshall has done the opposite."

"Like I said, he's a great guy. It takes a big man to recognize when he needs to change and to actually make that change. If we have to call on him Sunday, I have no doubt he'll be ready to compete on the biggest stage in the world."

"He says you taught him to see things this way. What is he referring to?"

"Big thinkers don't run from change. They embrace it."

We arrived at the hotel, but I had to know more about what Jay meant.

23

It was late and Jay was working sixteen-hour days to prepare for the biggest game of his career, but the man seemed to have boundless energy and he loved talking about the philosophy he felt so strongly about.

He invited me into the team hotel and after he signed a few autographs for fans waiting in the lobby, we went to the hotel restaurant where I joined Jay for a late-night burger.

"You mentioned, 'Big thinkers don't run from change,'" I said. "In Marshall's case, what choice did he have? It wasn't his decision to be benched. I'm sure he wished he could have avoided a change like that."

"**Change is going to happen, whether you choose for it to happen or not**," Jay said. "That's football and that's life; change is always happening. **Sometimes you actively decide to change something and sometimes you are forced to deal with changes outside of your control. But you always get to decide** how you *respond* to change.

"You can respond to change with big thinking or small thinking. **Big thinkers embrace change. They are willing to evolve and they are open to new ideas. They attack and adapt to the situation. They respond to change by making a positive change within themselves. This is often referred to as a** *growth* **mindset. They recognize they have the ability to adapt and change for the better. They choose to believe that something positive can come out of every forced change. They choose to believe that forced change isn't happening** *to* **them, it's happening** *for* **them.**

"Small thinkers, on the other hand, have a small and restrictive view about life. They want everything to stay the same. They are frightened by change. They have a limited, fixed mindset where they don't think they're capable of changing, expanding, or improving. They aren't open to new ideas or opportunities. When a change they don't like occurs, they respond with anger or self-pity. They close themselves off to new growth opportunities. Instead of adapting to the situation and considering how it could be positive or how they could grow from it, they catastrophize it and stubbornly refuse to adapt."

"Marshall told me he responded to being benched with a period of anger and self-pity," I said.

"Most of us respond to negative changes that way. At least at first. None of us like being forced to change when things have been going the way we want them to go. How long we allow ourselves to stay in that negative state of anger or self-pity is up to us. You have to catch yourself and reevaluate the situation, just like Marshall did. **You have to step back from the initial feelings of anger or from feeling sorry for yourself and say, 'How could this situation turn out to be a good thing for me? How can I *grow* into a stronger and better person because of this? What can I learn from this? What do I need to change about myself to adapt to this situation?'**

"When we ask ourselves questions like that, we force ourselves to grow. **The quicker you can change from a fixed mindset—where you don't think you can adapt or evolve—to a growth mindset—where you know you can adapt and improve—the more successful you will be.**

"**To think big is to have a growing, expanding mindset that embraces change. To think small is to have a fixed, limited mindset that is afraid of change.**"

I was quiet for a moment as I reflected on my own life.

"What is it?" Jay asked.

"I'm realizing how small I've been thinking when faced with change," I said. "The way you describe a fixed mindset—being afraid to change, being angry, wallowing in self-pity. Thinking smaller instead of bigger. That's exactly how I responded to losing my job. And I don't think I ever transitioned out of it. I'm stuck."

"That right there—thinking you're *stuck*—is a fixed mindset. You can change your mindset anytime you want. You can choose to start thinking big right now.

"Ask yourself questions like the ones I laid out. You lost a job you liked. How could that turn out to be a good thing for you?"

"I know I'm supposed to say something like, 'It could lead me to a better job, a better opportunity.' But it didn't. I never found a better job."

"Or, you could say, 'It gave me the opportunity to chase one of my other dreams—writing books—while looking for a new job. It allowed me to spend more time with my kids during a time when they were home and benefited from having their father around more. It led me to where I am right now, with unprecedented access to an NFL team as they prepare for the Super Bowl.' No matter the change, you can almost always find *something* good that can come from it. Of course, it's up to you to act on the opportunities the change is offering you.

"And even if you can't find something you're convinced is good about the change, you *can* always find ways the situation is helping you grow, learn, and become a better person. Surely, losing your job taught you empathy for people going through similar situations. Surely, you learned to be more resilient in the face of adversity, otherwise you wouldn't be here right now, still chasing your dream as a sportswriter. Surely, you learned to continue being a loving father and husband despite your career adversity; you learned to laugh, enjoy life, and care for the people close to you even while you were frustrated about your job situation—that builds character."

"I hadn't thought of it that way."

"But here's the most important question, Sean. Here's the question I'm not sure you've asked yourself ever since that setback three years ago: what do you need to change about yourself to adapt to the situation?"

I nodded. "You're right. I admit it; I haven't taken responsibility for what I need to change about myself. That's exactly why talking with Marshall was so inspiring to me. Two weeks after losing his starting job, he looked in the mirror and accepted responsibility for the changes he had to make. Three years after I lost my job, I still haven't done that."

"There's no time like the present," Jay said. "Here's the other thing about change. **No matter how good or bad things have been going for you, at some point, if you want to take that step to the next level of success, you're going to have to change something about yourself.**

"**Big thinkers are never satisfied. They are always building, always expanding, always chasing new and bigger goals.** I'm not saying they don't take the time to celebrate their success, enjoy life, and be grateful for what they have. That's a huge part of being happy and successful. What I'm saying is that **big thinkers never stop chasing a goal.** Man was created to pursue goals. We are goal-striving beings. **A person can't truly be happy without having a goal they are excited about chasing.** Once one goal is achieved, you have to set a new goal. That's what it means to think big. You keep raising the bar. You keep breaking through to the next level.

"**Your potential is limited only by what you *think* you can achieve. You have to break through any mental barriers you've set about what you're capable of.** Tear down those walls, break through to the next level. It's all in your mind.

"Small thinkers are always looking for ways to coast. They want to achieve a certain level they are initially satisfied with, and then they want to stay at that level. They don't want to change or stretch themselves. They don't want anything or anyone to disrupt where they are. That's why they get so rattled by change.

"**You're always either moving forward or moving backward. There is no in-between. The moment you try to *maintain* where you are, you'll start falling backwards, getting beat by those who are focused on moving forward.**

"You've got to always have a bigger goal in front of you. Something you're excited to chase after. That's one of the secrets to happiness. Too many people think the key to being happy is to reach a certain level and then stay there, but that leads to boredom and fear that someone is going to take what you have. **Happiness comes from the pursuit of something exciting.** I know it's a cliché to say, but it's the journey, not the destination, that brings us joy.

"Big thinkers embrace change and are never satisfied with where they are. They're always adapting and always moving forward, climbing higher, and charting new paths. To do that, you have to keep learning, growing, and expanding your thinking. You've got to keep asking yourself, 'How can I go further? How can I improve? How can I reach the next level? How can I achieve bigger goals or live a bigger, more fulfilling life?'

"The point I'm trying to make is, **whether you choose to change because you want to achieve a greater level of success or whether you're forced to change because situations outside of your control have been altered, the one thing you can be certain of is that constant change is necessary. So you might as well have a positive attitude towards it. Embrace it. Grow from it.**"

24

Thursday of Super Bowl week was a little less chaotic for the coaches and players. The game plans were in. The players practiced without pads to minimize injuries. Surprising to me, coaches and players alike seemed *looser* as the biggest game of their lives approached. Spirits were high. Observing the team, you would have no idea they were now 17.5-point underdogs and that pretty much everyone on press row expected Sunday to be one of the most lopsided Super Bowls in history.

During the late afternoon, I called Ethan. I had put it off as long as I could. He had texted me a few times to see how the story was coming along. He wanted to make sure he and I were *on the same page*, he wrote.

"How we looking?" Ethan asked. "Find anybody to sling dirt on their fearless leader?"

"No dirt," I said. "And I've talked to several of the bench guys now. Even had a long conversation with

Marshall Lewis. He gave me some off-the-record stuff, but nothing negative about Porter. I'm telling you, everyone I talk to seems to love the guy."

"They're saying that now. We'll see what everybody says after Sunday's beatdown. You sure you aren't handling everybody with kid gloves, Sean? More worried about making friends with these guys than getting the truth out of them?"

"Not at all," I said. "Getting to the truth is what I've been doing from the start."

Ethan sighed loud enough for me to hear it on the phone. "Okay, okay. We're going to have to do something different. Instead of a behind-the-scenes expose, you're going to have to make this story more about *your* perspective. You always wanted to be a columnist, right?"

"Absolutely," I said, excited about what I was hearing.

"Show me you can do it. Write the story from your vantage point, about everything you've seen. Paint yourself as the only cool head in the room. Work up the angle that Porter's got everyone brainwashed, even the backups and guys who should be questioning him."

My excitement faded as Ethan continued.

"Let your voice be heard," he said. "Make this story about how you walked into this Pollyanna environment and at first you bought into it, but then you saw it for what it was: a big show hiding the reality of a low-talent team on the luckiest streak in NFL history. Maybe play up that Porter is stuck in the past with his, 'just put your mind to it and you can accomplish anything' routine."

I had dreamt about being a national sports columnist, someone who could share his opinion with the sports world. But Ethan wanted me to express an opinion that wasn't mine.

"You can do something like that, right?" Ethan said.

Now it was my turn to sigh. "That's not what I see happening."

"Then you need to look harder. Sean, if you want to play in the big leagues, you've got to put yourself out there and do things that may not be popular with the people you've interviewed. If you want to be a big-time columnist, this is what you have to do. You've got to take off those rose-colored glasses and run with the big dogs. Can you handle that? Are you ready for the big leagues?"

After several rounds of back-and-forth, Ethan persuaded me to take a swing at the story the way he wanted. I saw where he was coming from. He hired me to write a specific type of story. I had agreed to do it. And now it was too late to hire another writer.

Ethan was also very good at making me question myself. (Of course, as an unemployed writer struggling with self-doubt for the last three years, that wasn't too hard to do.)

"What will people think if your first national column for us is a glowing feature on how transformative Porter's message is and then his team gets blown out of the stadium on Sunday?" Ethan had asked.

It was a fair point.

The story was supposed to go live the Saturday night before the Super Bowl. It was supposed to be something everyone would be talking about on Sunday morning. How St. Louis opened its doors to a writer, gave him an all-access look at how this Cinderella team was preparing for the Super Bowl, and revealed what was *really* taking place behind the scenes. It had to be provocative.

A story about how Coach Porter won over a skeptical sportswriter wouldn't bring the attention Ethan wanted. "It sure as hell wouldn't be worth the two weeks' pay we agreed to," Ethan said.

I was stuck. This was the chance I had been waiting for. A chance to be a national sports columnist. A chance to have the entire nation talking about my column. A chance to hit the *big* time.

A feel-good story about a team that in all likelihood was about to be embarrassed in front of a worldwide audience would not only fail to generate the buzz *The Cheap Seats* needed, but it would also make me look like a naive reporter who had bought into a foolish message.

If I didn't take this story in the direction Ethan wanted it to go, not only would I be burning bridges with *The Cheap Seats*, but I'd also be blowing my opportunity to be a national columnist, something I'd been dreaming about since I was a kid.

This was my opportunity to *think big*.

25

The more I thought about writing the column in a critical tone, the more I could see angles that would work.

Jay was a good guy; my column would make that clear. But I could still question whether he and his coaching style belonged in the NFL. Was he treating his players fairly? Was it right to bench a proven, veteran quarterback because you liked the backup's attitude better? Was it responsible to teach people that the reason they lost in sports or in life was because they weren't thinking big enough? Was Jay an egomaniac who saw himself superior to other coaches because he "thought bigger" than they did?

Once I went looking for a more cynical angle to the story, it wasn't hard to find. After all, news networks have been doing this kind of thing for years. Why couldn't I do it for one story?

I planned on quietly exiting the local college

campus the Stallions were borrowing for practice without asking Jay any more questions on Thursday. I had enough for my feature and I didn't want to feel any guiltier about the negative slant I was preparing to give it.

My plan changed after Jay met with the media that evening. One exchange piqued my interest.

A reporter asked Jay what a Super Bowl victory would mean not only to the Stallions organization, but to the city of St. Louis.

"That's not something we take lightly," he said. "Part of our think-big philosophy is playing for a bigger purpose. I tell our guys all the time, 'You're playing for something bigger.'"

I had heard Jay repeat that exact phrase several times over my two weeks following the team. He said it to players and coaches. I never asked him about it because I assumed he was referring to the Super Bowl itself, playing in the biggest game of the season.

"When I say that," Jay continued with the reporter, "I'm talking about attaching yourself to something bigger than you, something bigger than this game. We're not playing for ourselves. We're playing for each other. We're playing for each other's families.

We're playing for the city of St. Louis and all the Stallion fans who are connected to us. I'd like to think we're also representing all the underdogs out there who are daring to dream big. We're playing for a bigger purpose than just ourselves, and we have been from the start. **You can accomplish so much more when you connect to a purpose bigger than yourself.**

"So yeah, we believe we're playing for St. Louis and it would mean the world to us to bring the city and the community a Lombardi Trophy."

None of the reporters followed up. They had the soundbite they wanted. Not me. I needed more. Something about what he said didn't sit right with me.

26

After Jay's Thursday press conference, he went back to his hotel where one of the suites had been converted to his own personal office, complete with a giant TV for breaking down film. Coaches can never get enough film.

I knocked on his door and asked if he had time for a few follow-up questions before I headed home. He greeted me warmly and told me to have a seat. I sat down in one of the lush hotel chairs and turned on my recorder.

"Can I be frank, for a moment?" I said.

"As frank as you want to be," Jay said with a smile as he adjusted his *STL* cap and leaned back in his desk chair.

"Some people have accused you of having, well, a big ego."

"Uh-oh, it's a question from 'some people' again."

I forced a smile of my own, but continued with the

uncomfortable line of questioning.

"Going back to your days as a college coach, you've had critics who say your *Think Big to Win Big* motto is just a branding tool for you. They say it's a way to promote yourself; that your message is all about making *you* stand out. With this in mind, there's something you said at tonight's press conference that, if I'm doing my job as a reporter, I've got to call you out on."

"I'm curious where you're going with this," Jay said. "Fire away."

"You were talking about playing for a bigger purpose. Attaching yourself to a bigger purpose. How you want to believe your team is playing not only for St. Louis, but for *all* the underdogs out there."

"That's right. We know we're giant underdogs. We know nobody expected us to be here. I think underdogs everywhere can relate to that."

"Well, for someone who has been accused of having a self-promoting ego, don't you think people could hear that and think, 'Who does this guy think he is, claiming to represent anyone who has ever had a big dream? Who made him the spokesman for *all* the underdogs out there? This is a classic example of Jay

Porter thinking he is a bigger deal than he is.'"

I was trying to push Jay's buttons. I wanted to see if I could get a rise out of him, maybe make him angry enough to snap at me and give me something confrontational I could use in my story. I was poking the bear to see how it would react.

Jay grinned as he adjusted his cap. "First off, I do think I'm bigger than most people think I am. That's not arrogance; that's confidence. If I had let other people determine what I was capable of, I would not be in the position I'm in right now, living my dream as a head coach in the NFL. I can't let anyone else decide how big or small I'm allowed to think.

"The great sports psychologist, Bob Rotella, once said, 'Champions understand that they must be confident to a point that some people might find offensive.' If you're confident, you *are* going to offend the people who think you don't belong or don't have what it takes.

"I know there are lots of people who think I don't belong in the NFL. I'm not your typical tight-lipped coach. I love what I'm doing and I'm not afraid to let people know that. I know my style isn't for everyone, especially in this league. But you know what? There were lots of people who said I didn't belong as a head coach in college, either. All my life, people have been telling me to tamp down my goals, to be more realistic, to wait my turn, to turn it down a notch. And I'm sure a lot of those people are offended that I chose to not listen to them and dared to aim higher and think bigger of myself than they thought I should.

"But that's *their* problem, not mine. If me believing in myself means I have an ego, so be it. **I can't let other people determine how highly or lowly I'm allowed to think of myself. That's up to me. And I choose to think big!**

"That's confidence, not arrogance. And I want every one of my players and coaches to think the exact same way: that we're all capable of much more than others think we are.

"As for saying we represent the city of St. Louis and underdogs everywhere, I don't think that's arrogance. That's humility. It's a reminder that our purpose goes beyond just what's in it for us. If we succeed, so do many other people—some in big ways and some in small ways, but the reality is that a lot of people we've never met have a vested interest in what we do.

"It's also a reminder that we serve a greater

community and people all over the world are watching what we're doing and how we're doing it. How we carry ourselves matters. We're setting an example. How we handle success and how we handle failure, people are watching and learning from us because of the big stage we've been given.

"That's not my ego talking; that's reality. Right or wrong, people look up to these players and how they carry themselves matters. Because of my position, I know some people are looking up to me, also. That's an awesome responsibility and I don't want our players or coaches or myself ever taking it for granted.

"**Every high-achieving organization or team I've studied has recognized that their actions, their attitudes, their successes, and their failures all affect a lot more people than just those who are members of the team.** You have to embrace that fact. Don't let it overwhelm you. Be proud of it. It's an awesome responsibility you've been blessed with.

"The successful CEO or salesperson knows the products they sell are impacting not just their customers, but also their customers' families and their communities. The successful high school coach knows how much his players' families and the rest of the community care about how the team represents them. The successful parent knows their kids are watching closely how they handle that financial or medical crisis. *All* **great teams realize they're a part of something bigger than themselves. They're playing for a bigger purpose.**

"Tell me, Sean, do you think that's an ego-driven philosophy?"

27

"I hadn't thought of it that way," I said. "Still though, taken out of context, that soundbite from today's presser about you representing all the underdogs out there, it could be construed—"

"How somebody *construes* something about me is not really in my control," Jay said. "I focus on only the things I have control over.

"The thing I want you to see is how this purpose-driven mentality affects every single thing you do. It's not just for guys in the NFL or on sports teams. Everybody should be attaching themselves to a bigger purpose. They should be looking to build bigger alliances. They should be thinking bigger about themselves *and* the larger team they're a part of. Keeping this in mind makes you much more effective at your job."

"How so?"

"When you attach yourself to a cause bigger than

yourself, it removes your own egotism from the mission. It forces you to say, 'Okay, what is the best action I can take for my team, my community, my family; even if it might not be the best thing for me personally?'

"If you know you're fighting for a bigger purpose than your own personal gain, it reminds you not only that what you're doing is helping others, but that *they* are also helping *you*. You're not alone. You're fighting for them and they're fighting for you. Your success is their success and their success is your success. We're all in this together.

"Being a part of a bigger team means we're all humble enough to ask each other for help. We pick up our teammates when they're down and let them do the same for us. We don't close ourselves off in times of trouble. We're open and honest with each other because we're all fighting for a bigger purpose. That makes it easier to achieve difficult goals.

"Big thinkers build big alliances. They know they can achieve much more as a team than as an individual, so they're always thinking about what's best for *us* — as a team, as a community, as a family. They ask themselves, 'What's the best way to serve the bigger purpose?'

"Small thinkers think *me* instead of *we*. They're focused on what's in it for them and they're willing to sabotage the team's mission if it means more individual success for themselves.

"Sometimes they do this on purpose, like when a coworker goes behind someone's back and starts spreading rumors about them to try to make themselves look better. But usually, these small thinkers are sabotaging the team's mission without even realizing it, like when they whine or complain or have a bad attitude on days when they're not feeling great. That negativity spreads to others.

"In my line of work, this type of small thinking could be as simple as a player telling himself, 'It's okay to take a few plays off, nobody will notice, somebody else will pick up the slack.' When you don't do your job on a single play, that can—and often does—mean the difference between winning and losing.

"**Big thinkers know that everything they do affects the entire team. Small thinkers are mostly focused on themselves and they tend to be short-term focused.** They convince themselves their effort in one practice or on one play won't matter all that much.

"Do you see the difference it makes when you attach yourself to a bigger purpose?"

I nodded, realizing Jay was once again coaching *me*. He wasn't concerned with defending his statement from the press conference. He was concerned with showing me how his philosophy could improve not just his and his team's chances of success, but mine as well.

28

"I see how this type of thinking is helpful for a team," I said. "But couldn't it also create a lot more pressure? For example, I agree with you that everything I do is affecting my family. That's my team. They are my greater purpose. But that's also why it's so gut-wrenching to fail. I know I'm letting them down."

"How you *respond* to failure is having the greatest impact on them," Jay said. "Ask any coach's spouse. They'll tell you they're going through every victory and defeat right along with the coach. They hear the public criticisms, they worry when you worry, they know the stakes and they pack up and move with you when you get fired. It's not a lot different than the insecurity that comes with many jobs except, as a coach, it all happens in a very public way.

"That used to destroy me. We'd lose a game and I'd be convinced I was about to get fired. I'd be a nervous wreck, and that made my wife a nervous wreck. One night, after a bad loss, I was telling her how worried I was and how sorry I was for putting her and our kids in this position. She turned to me and said, 'Jay, I can handle the ups and downs of this life if *you* can.'

"Talk about a wakeup call. It made me realize she was going through the ups and downs of life with me, but what she cared about more than anything was how I *handled* those ups and downs. She wasn't asking me to go undefeated. She just wanted me to be happy and do my best at what I loved doing. She wanted me to stay positive and resilient. If I could do that, no matter what happened, our family would be fine.

"That's something to keep in mind whenever you get frustrated by adversity—those times when you're working your way up, having to take jobs you don't like, opening up a rejection letter and then still sitting down to work on your next article or book proposal—every step you take matters to your family and the people who care about you. They want to see you moving forward regardless of the setbacks and they want to see you doing it with a positive attitude.

"That's why it's so important to stay positive and resilient even when you're not getting the results you want. Your family is watching how you react. Your kids especially are learning from you. They want you to stay positive. That's what is most important to them.

"Yes, being part of a bigger purpose brings with it bigger responsibilities. But remember, the most important responsibility you have is the effort and attitude you carry yourself with. How you respond to adversity, in particular, is going to have the greatest impact on your team. As long as you keep fighting, stay positive, and refuse to quit, you'll never let them down."

"That is good advice," I said, feeling guilty about times when I reacted to adversity by whining, complaining, and wallowing in self-pity for way too long.

As we talked, I realized once again that what initially sounded like an off-the-cuff comment at a press conference was actually part of a much bigger, well-thought-out point in Jay's philosophy.

The size of your thinking determines the size of your success.

Big thinkers set big goals and expect to achieve them.

Be bigger than your problems.

Big thinkers dare to dream big and take risks.

Big thinkers embrace change and are never satisfied.

Small, consistent action leads to big, massive success.

Big thinkers attach themselves to a bigger purpose.

These weren't quick quips that floated into Jay's head, as an outside observer like myself might assume. They were crucial parts of his *Think Big to Win Big* philosophy. He had put in *years* thinking about each component and applying it to his life and his teams.

There was very little Jay said that he hadn't personally researched and tested in his life before teaching those lessons to his team or anyone else who cared enough to ask.

29

I woke up early Friday morning and began finalizing the feature column that would shape my career. It was the opportunity I'd been waiting all my life for. The chance to write a column for a national sports publication after spending nearly two weeks with an NFL team and its coaches as they prepared for the Super Bowl. Most writers *never* get an opportunity like this. I could not blow it.

It was time to make the decision that would make or break my professional life.

Would I write the snarky, cynical, provocative article Ethan wanted me to write? Or, would I bare my soul and write about how I saw Jay Porter inspiring a team to overachieve, and how he was inspiring *me* to change my way of thinking?

When I left Jay's office the night before, I didn't think I'd be able to write the column Ethan wanted. The image he wanted portrayed didn't mesh with the image I had of Jay and the way he ran his team.

I spent a restless night falling in and out of sleep as I struggled with my conscience. If I couldn't write the column Ethan wanted, what was I going to do?

Finally, in the early-morning hours, I had an epiphany.

Do I really believe the things Jay says? Or do I just WANT to believe them? Do I really believe the size of my thinking determines the size of my success? Do I really believe I've struggled to find work the last three years because I've had a negative attitude? If that was the case, how did this opportunity of a lifetime fall into my lap? It happened when I wasn't thinking big. I wasn't being more positive, enthusiastic, or purposeful with my actions. It just … happened. Right out of the blue. Pure luck. Nothing more. Isn't it more truthful to admit that life usually just happens to us, whether we're thinking big or not? Isn't it naive to believe I can somehow control my fate with my thinking?

I had been cynical and angry for so long; it was easy to snap back into a negative thought pattern, especially during early-morning, sleep-deprived hours.

Of course, the most important question I was asking myself was a self-centered one. *Do I really want to throw away the opportunity of a lifetime to defend a man and a philosophy I wasn't even sure I believed in?*

As I continued to question everything Jay had taught me over the last two weeks, I slowly started to convince myself that telling people, "If you think big, you'll win big," is not only unproven, it's irresponsible.

Sure, I could look back on my life and find times when it seemed as though positive results followed a positive attitude, and there were times when I'd get into a negative funk and it seemed like one bad thing happened after another. But there were plenty of other times when my experiences *didn't* seem to follow any specific attitude.

As my cynicism rose, so did my confidence in writing the column Ethan wanted me to write.

By the time I started working on the piece, I had convinced myself Jay's philosophy was at best a silly and unproven one, and at worst an irresponsible and dangerous one. I had bought into his ideas because they were exciting and he was a charismatic leader. *Now*, I told myself, *I see the truth*.

I wrote my column as fast as I could, not wanting to allow my conscience to question my motives. I portrayed Jay the way Ethan wanted him portrayed. I shared an inside look at St. Louis' practice routines and preparation for the Super Bowl, including my own personal opinions on what I observed along the way. These opinions were delivered with a cynical, smart-aleck tone.

As I wrote, there were times when that voice inside told me I wasn't being fair. It said I was forcing myself to take a position I didn't agree with.

I squelched that voice. I wasn't going to let Jay's likeable personality and persuasive motivational skills slant my thinking any longer.

Besides, what choice did I have if I wanted to land my dream job? It was Ethan's way or the highway. I had to do the job the boss was paying me to do, so I might as well get on board with the same line of thinking.

I finished the column and read through it multiple times, cringing at a few parts where I had taken some unfair shots at Jay and his philosophy.

But that's the type of stuff that gets attention, I told myself.

I poked fun at several of Jay's core principles, despite the fact that those very same principles had forced me to do some serious soul searching over the past two weeks. Now, I was questioning it all.

Think big to win big? What happens when you think big and get embarrassed on the biggest sports stage there is?

Set big expectations and expect big success to come your way? That sounds great until you get blindsided by some obstacle you never expected.

Dream big and take risks? Reckless advice, if you ask me. Tell that to the entrepreneur who lost his life savings chasing his dream.

Small, consistent action leads to big success if you persist and keep the larger goal in mind? Sure, Jay, until it doesn't. As you're going to see on Sunday, sometimes your best just isn't good enough.

The most important factor determining your success or failure is the attitude you choose to have? Maybe in Fantasyland, but not in the real world. Those lines might work with susceptible college kids, but this is the NFL. It's time to grow up, Jay.

Shot after shot I took, letting the cynic in me slam each of Jay's fundamental beliefs. I convinced myself Jay was just like those motivational gurus you see on the Internet, pumping you up with false hope.

I told myself I wasn't being *that* harsh. Sure, there were a few cheap shots thrown at Jay, but I kept them good-natured. I even made sure to mention what a great guy I thought he was. I may not have been buying his teachings, but I still liked and appreciated him.

How quickly I had convinced myself to believe things I was not so sure of when doing so would just so happen to bring me instant financial and professional gains.

When I finished the column, I asked Jenny for her feedback. As she read it, I didn't hear any of the laughs I hoped to hear. Not a single courtesy chuckle.

When she finished, she looked at me and said, "I don't get it. This doesn't sound like the guy you've been telling me about every night for the past two weeks."

"Is it too harsh?" I asked.

"Why does it have to be harsh at all?"

"This is what Ethan wants. It's supposed to be kind of funny, kind of snarky."

"Why can't it just be … honest? You've been telling me what a great guy this coach is, how much he's changing your outlook and making you realize it's time for us to start thinking bigger. And I've seen the change in your mood since you've been around him. You're dreaming again. You're excited again. Why isn't any of that in this story? It's like you're downplaying the impact this coach is making on everyone, including *you*."

"I got excited about the job and bought into his message without questioning it. I see that now. As much as I like the guy, his team is going to get destroyed on Sunday. With the access I've had, we need to be able to tell the nation why it's going to happen. I can't make the story about me and I can't hype him up. That's not what people want to read."

"*I* would want to read that. I was anxious to learn more about what he was teaching you. This story basically mocks the poor guy for trying to do things different."

"You don't get it," I said with a condescending shake of my head. "I'm not mocking him. I'm pointing out the problems with his leadership style. Trust me, you'll see what I mean when you see what happens Sunday. You asked me to be honest, that's what I'm doing. I can't let my personal feelings cloud the truth about what's really going on."

Jenny studied me for a moment, then shrugged. "Well, if this is *really* the truth about what he's like…"

I looked away. "I might be taking a few unfair shots. But you know what? I'm sick and tired of being unemployed. This is the story I've been hired to write."

"But is it the truth? Is it something you feel good about doing?"

"It's the story I've been hired to write."

30

I debated with Jenny for another ten minutes or so. Mostly, it was me trying to convince her — and myself — I was being fair with my column. The more I argued my position, the more I convinced myself I was right. It's funny how we can force ourselves to see only what we want to see.

Right or wrong, this was the column I had to write if I wanted to become the next national columnist for *The Cheap Seats*.

But there was still one more thing I had to do before sending my column to Ethan.

I went to the campus where the Stallions were headquartered for Super Bowl week and caught the end of their Friday practice. They were going through red zone and goal line situations without pads. The team was in good spirits, but you could sense a more serious tone. The biggest game of their lives was just two days away. Despite being huge underdogs, St.

Louis was locked in. They believed they were going to shock the world.

For a moment, I thought to myself, *What if these guys actually win? What if the experts are wrong? What if they really do pull off the greatest upset in modern Super Bowl history? My column would look ridiculous.*

Nah, you're being silly, Sean. Of course, they're going to be hyped and focused. Of course, they believe in themselves right now. But they are outmatched at virtually every position. There's no way everyone could be so wrong about them. Maybe they'll find a way to keep it close, at best, but this game has annihilation written all over it.

Practice ended and Jay addressed the team, telling them how excited he was about the opportunity in front of them. He told them they were in control of their destiny. He told them to think big, win big. It was stuff they'd heard numerous times before, but it still got everyone fired up. Jay's enthusiasm was contagious and it affected everyone on the team.

As they walked off the field, I caught Jay's attention.

"Could I get a quick word, Coach?"

Jay looked at his watch. "Sure, what's up?"

I led him a good 15 yards away from everyone else. I didn't want anyone overhearing what I was about to say.

"I want to thank you for opening your door to me the way you have. And for taking so much time to, well, coach me up and try to help me get my fire back. I can tell you really care, and I appreciate that. I have a feeling this story is going to be the biggest story of my career and it would not have happened without your help."

"I've enjoyed talking with you, Sean, I really have. I believe your future is in your hands and things are going to go really well for you if you start thinking bigger about who you are and what you can accomplish."

"Right. I also want to tell you good luck on Sunday. I won't be bugging you anymore. I've got everything I need for the story."

"You're not coming to the game?"

"The story will already be published."

"No follow-up? I put you down for a media credential. You're not going to pass up a sideline pass to the Super Bowl, are you?"

His kindness was making me feeling lower and lower about myself.

"Actually, Jay, I don't think you'll to want to see

me after the story publishes."

He wrinkled his eye brows and adjusted his cap with a quick motion, looking both confused and adrenalized at the same time. "What do you mean?"

I took a deep breath and shifted my eyes away. I did my best to force a half-smile. "The boss wants this column to be—what's the word I'm looking for?—kind of … *funny*. It's not supposed to be too serious. The type of stuff that drives traffic, it's all a little edgy, a little snarky."

"Something tells me I'm not going to think it's very funny."

I forced a laugh that sounded as disingenuous as I felt. "No, no, it's nothing controversial. Nothing that will get anybody in trouble. It's just probably not what you're expecting."

"What are you trying to tell me, Sean?"

Jay folded his muscular arms and gave me an impatient look. He was tired of me beating around the bush.

"There are going to be some things in there you don't like. Things that make you and all that think-big stuff sound … a little silly, I guess. I wanted to tell you this in advance. Man-to-man."

Jay smiled, as though he was amused by the situation. "You want to apologize in advance for what you're about to publish about me? Something like that?"

I nodded. "Something like that."

Jay playfully swatted me on the shoulder. "You've got to do what you've got to do. Frankly, I don't care what people write about me, as long as it's the truth. And even if it isn't, I've got bigger things to focus on, like this little thing called the Super Bowl. What I *do* care about is you knowing I believe everything I preach. And I hope you do too, Sean, because I truly believe it can change your life."

"I don't doubt your sincerity. I never have, and I make that clear in the story. I'm just not sure *I* can buy into all of it."

No sense in hiding my thoughts any longer; they were going to be published for the world to see. I might as well come clean and let Jay know exactly what he could expect to see in the column. This wasn't going to be easy.

31

"All week long, I've been struggling with how to write this column," I said. "I went back and forth, wrestling with myself about what to say. In my two weeks with you and the team, I didn't find any controversy or shocking revelations that would get the sports world talking. What I found was one of the most positive people I've ever met. A leader who gets people excited about the future. A leader who is passionate, energetic, and enthusiastic. A leader who makes you believe in the impossible.

"I'll be honest, Jay, for most of the past two weeks I've been buying into your message. I've been wondering if the reason my life has been so crappy the last three years is because I'm not thinking big enough or positive enough or whatever. I've been telling myself I need to change the way I'm thinking.

"But last night, it hit me. I don't think I believe what you believe. It's too simplistic to think we become what we believe, or that the size of our thinking determines the size of our success, or that if we want to be more successful, we just need to think bigger and be more positive. That all sounds nice. It's exciting. It makes us *think* we're in control of our destinies. But we're not.

"Last night, I reflected on my life and realized we actually control very little of what happens to us, regardless of how positive or negative we are. Here I am with the biggest opportunity of my career, and it happened randomly. It had nothing to do with me thinking bigger. It happened because another writer, who I've never even met, left the job and I happened to be living where this year's Super Bowl is being played. That's it. Completely random. Nothing but luck. In fact, I had been in a pretty negative state of mind right up until I got the call that offered me this job.

"You see, Jay, I realized last night that life is really one big crapshoot, where some people get lucky and some people don't. And that makes me wonder if *you* might have lucked into the position you're in. I wonder if all this *Think Big to Win Big* talk is hiding the fact that this team did nothing more than fall into one of the luckiest streaks in pro football history.

"And I wonder what happens when that luck runs out. I wonder what happens to you and these players if you think big and end up *losing* big on the biggest stage there is, like everyone expects to happen on Sunday.

"It's easy to wear positivity on your sleeve when everything is going right, but what happens if you fail in embarrassing fashion? What happens to the super-talented quarterback who got benched because his coach thinks he 'wasn't thinking big enough?' What happens to all the young players who bought into the idea that everything will turn out great as long as they stay positive and think big? What happens when you come face to face with a problem that really is a lot bigger than you and the world smashes you down, takes away everything you wanted, and leaves you feeling hopeless with nobody to help you out no matter how big or positive you try to think? What then?

"Isn't your message—*if you think big, you'll win big*—nothing more than self-deception?"

The gloves were off. I was ranting away, unleashing all my doubts and criticisms. I half-expected Jay to shake his head and walk away. After all, he had been nothing but kind to me and here I was pretty much mocking the principles he lived by.

But Jay didn't walk away. He didn't show any anger, either.

Turns out, he was anxious to respond.

32

Jay took a step back and smiled again. "Wow. You came out swinging today."

"I'm not trying to offend you, but this is his is how I feel."

"I'm not offended at all," Jay said. "But I do think your portrayal of what I've said is inaccurate. I've never implied that only good things can happen to you as long as you think big or that only bad things can happen to you if you think small. That's not what I've told you, and I think you know that.

"What this is really about is you making the decision not to believe what I believe, which is your choice. I can't make anyone else believe things they don't want to believe.

"We all get to choose what we believe. Our beliefs make us who we are and determine what we achieve. The bigger you believe, the bigger you will achieve. I believe that with all my heart, but I can't make you

201

or anyone else believe the same thing. Everyone gets to choose their own beliefs.

"Sadly, most people see the world as 'one big crapshoot,' just like you said. They feel they have no control over their destinies. There was a time when I thought the same way.

"You see, my old man was one of the most negative people you could ever meet. He hated his job. He didn't like his life. He drank himself into the hospital when I was only eight and he left our family when I was ten. His lessons to me were always the same: 'Don't trust anyone. Life is unfair. Don't get your hopes up because you'll only be disappointed.' Those messages were imbedded in me at a young age. It tainted my view of the world.

"My views started to change when I entered high school. My football coach challenged all those beliefs. He told me my future was up to me. He told me life is what you make it. He said you can achieve anything you put your mind to. He told me God had big plans for my future."

I noticed Jay's eyes misting up as he thought about his old coach.

"Slowly but surely, I started testing those beliefs,"

Jay said. "I looked at my dad's life and saw where his negative view of the world had gotten him. I looked at my coach—a happy, successful, passionate guy who had won a couple of state titles—and saw where his positive attitude had gotten him. Who was I going to follow? Whose beliefs did I want to emulate? Right before my senior year in high school, I realized it was time to make a choice, and the choice was clear.

"I started challenging myself to think positively, to think bigger. Anybody who told me I couldn't achieve something; I refused to listen. My senior year, I went from riding the bench to all-district. In college, I went from walk-on to all-conference. You know my story. *None* of it would have happened if I hadn't changed my attitude, the way I viewed the world, back in high school. And like I told you before, I made another big change in thinking after my playing days were over.

"The point is, we all get to choose what we believe and how we think. You can take the cynical, fatalistic view, convinced you have very little control over where you end up. That's easy to do. It's what most people do. But if you choose to go down that route, I promise you will end up less successful and less happy in life.

"You can disagree with my beliefs. I've been hearing the same criticisms you laid out at virtually every stop in my career. I get it. I'm an easy target because I wear my beliefs on my sleeve. But honestly, I don't care what the critics think. All I can worry about is what *I* think and whether I'm effectively teaching my team the beliefs I know to be true, the beliefs I know will help us succeed.

"All I can do is share what has worked for me. I've lived my life both ways. **I spent years thinking small and petty, and I've spent years thinking big and optimistic. I know which attitude produces the results I want.** The think-big principles I preach have worked for me and they'll work for anyone else who chooses to implement them. I know this because I've seen it happen for hundreds of my players, coaches, and associates. **Change the way you think and you'll change your life.**

"Every objection you've raised is nothing more than an opinion, and everyone is entitled to their own opinions. How you choose to think becomes self-fulfilling. If you choose to think the world is a negative, hopeless place you have no control over, you'll end up living a life that confirms that viewpoint. If you choose to see the world as a positive, exciting place with unlimited opportunities, believing you can make a difference with your choices and that your attitude is the single most important choice you can make, you'll end up living a life that confirms that.

"**It's up to you to decide what kind of attitude you will have and what kind of life you're going to live.**

"Here's what I know. The size of one's thinking *does* determine the size of one's success. How you see yourself *does* determine the person you become. Optimists *do* outperform pessimists. I've seen that happen again and again in my own life and there are decades of psychological studies that prove it as well.

"Does all this mean if you just think positive enough, nothing bad will ever happen to you? Does it mean if you think big enough, you'll go through life undefeated? Of course not. There are always going to be some factors outside of your control.

"But here's the key. **It's those times when life blindsides you with adversity when it becomes most important for you to respond with a big, optimistic, growth-oriented attitude.** It's that big attitude that tells you you're bigger than your problems. You're too big to stay down."

"But what do you say to the person who thinks big, chases their dreams, and ends up losing the big game or the big job or whatever?" I said. "Doesn't that make all this positive thinking a waste of time?"

"Sometimes you can do all the right things and still lose. That's life. But it's during those times of adversity when it's most crucial to keep a positive attitude. You call on that positive attitude to pick yourself back up. There's always a next game and a new opportunity. Positive thinking won't protect you from ever having anything bad happen to you, but it will fuel a much faster rebound when something bad does happen.

"I don't preach magical thinking. I've never told anyone that as long as they're positive they'll never encounter any problems. I tell them what I'm telling you: **how you respond to problems will determine where you end up.** *You* get to choose whether you respond with a positive, I-can-find-a-way-through-this attitude or a negative, what's-the-point-in-trying attitude. Big thinkers respond with a positive attitude and that's why they win big in the game of life.

"We might lose on Sunday. We're playing a great team and I know a lot of people are predicting we'll get blown out of the stadium. If that happens, I'll be disappointed, I'll be upset, I'll be questioning our preparation and our decisions, learning from our mistakes. But I won't be devastated to the point of despair. I won't be quitting on my dreams. I won't be mad at myself for expecting to win because I know those big expectations are what got us here in the first place. Our team will get right back up and start thinking big about the future. **Big thinking won't guarantee you reach every single goal you set, but it will ensure you achieve much more than you would as a small thinker.**

"I can't stand here and tell you that you control each and every thing that happens to you. That would be a lie. What I can tell you is that you control how *most* things turn out. It's your response to what happens that determines where you end up.

"You have control over your life. That scares a lot of people. They'd rather not believe that. They'd rather blame luck or fate or other people for where they are. They'd rather not take responsibility for their results. That's small thinking.

"**Small thinkers go through life waiting for someone or something to change their lives for them.**

Big thinkers are too busy changing their lives for themselves.

"To passively go through life believing it's a crapshoot you have no control over is the most hopeless approach I can imagine. That fatalistic view of the world only sets you up for underachievement and despair. I hope *you're* not going down that road, Sean.

"Write whatever article you want about me, but don't spend the rest of your life thinking small. You'll limit yourself and I don't want to see that happen to you. **You've got unlimited potential inside you. The only way to unleash it is to think big.**"

Jay cared very little about how my story would end up, but he cared a great deal about how *I* would end up.

Still, he hadn't answered the one question that had triggered my epiphany and made me question everything he was preaching.

33

The Southern California sun was setting on us. I knew my time with Jay was running out. He had to get back to his team and I had to send my article to Ethan before my 7 p.m. deadline.

"I'll admit my criticisms are subjective," I said, "based on my own beliefs. Maybe you're right and I'm wrong. I'll concede that. But you have to admit that plain old luck plays a major role in determining life's winners and losers. Can't you admit your team has been *extremely* lucky this season? Can't you admit luck—being in the right place at the right time—has played a significant role in your career? I know it has in mine. I took a job at a paper that went bankrupt; that's bad luck. I got this assignment because I happened to be in the right place at the right time; that's good luck. I wasn't thinking positive when I got this job offer. It was quite the opposite."

"Sure, luck plays a role in life," Jay said. "But again,

whether you encounter good or bad luck, what matters most is how you *respond* to it. Big, positive thinkers will look for ways to turn good luck into winning streaks and bad luck into new opportunities. Small, negative thinkers will find ways to squander great opportunities or turn bad luck into extended losing streaks. I see this happen all the time. **We all tend to find more of what we go looking for.**

"That's why positive thinkers experience more good luck than negative thinkers. Good things tend to happen to people who expect good things to happen. I can't explain exactly why this happens, but it does. When you expect good luck, you tend to find it. When you expect bad luck, it tends to find you."

"Then how do you explain me getting the biggest opportunity of my career when I was *expecting* more disappointment?"

"First off, if you're still expecting disappointment, I hope you will change your expectations. I don't want you turning this great opportunity of yours into a greater disappointment."

At that comment, I felt my stomach drop just a bit. Was I about to blow this opportunity? Was I sabotaging myself with a cynical attitude? I didn't think long about it because Jay had more to say.

"The other thing I'd say about that is, well …" Jay adjusted his cap and looked up to the orange and pink sky. He wasn't sure if he wanted to say what he was about to say. "This is a little more personal than I usually get."

He had my attention. I didn't press him. I waited until he was ready to continue.

"**Big thinkers are big believers**," he said. "**Most of the great achievers I've studied have *big* faith.** They believe in divine intervention. They believe in a big and powerful God who wants to help them. They might not always call it 'God,' but they believe in a higher power that wants them to be successful.

"I believe God knows a lot more than we do. I also believe God loves me and wants me to be happy and successful. I believe God meets me halfway in life. If I think big and do the very best I can, he will step in and finish the job in the best way possible, which might not always be the way *I* wanted things to go. I trust that God knows better than I do. That viewpoint brings me a lot of peace.

"I'm not trying to push a particular religious view

on anyone. But I've learned that big thinkers believe big faith is required to achieve greatness. **Big thinkers believe in something much bigger than themselves and they're willing to trust this higher power.** I believe that higher power is God and he can take each of us so much further than we could ever go on our own. He knows things we can't know. We have to trust that."

"I can respect that," I said. "But how exactly does all this answer my question about luck?"

"What you call random good luck, I call divine intervention. Even though I personally believe negative thoughts and actions can sometimes block God's best from our lives, I think he keeps reaching out to us, giving us opportunities to excel again and again. It's our job to respond to those opportunities in the right way."

"You think I received this job offer not because of luck, but because of divine intervention?"

"I do," Jay said. "And I also believe when things don't turn out the way we want them to, God is there to help us move forward. I believe God can bring a greater good out of every bad thing that happens to us. That's what it means to have faith. That's why, win or lose on Sunday, I'm going to keep enjoying my life. I'm going to keep moving forward. I'm going to keep thinking big. I'm going to keep expecting great things to come my way in the future.

"I don't know if I could believe what I believe without having this kind of faith. My faith in God is something I *choose* to believe. It's a belief that empowers me.

"I can't answer all of life's great theological questions, but I can choose to believe. I can choose to have faith in a higher power. I can choose to believe there is something much greater and wiser than me guiding me through life.

"This faith brings me peace. It allows me to think bigger, aim higher, and achieve much more than I ever could if I felt like I was on my own."

Jay took a step back and smiled, as if he was stepping out of a momentary trance.

"Okay, end of sermon," he said with a grin as he checked his watch. "I'm not trying to convert you and I didn't expect to go down this path. I'm just answering your questions as honestly as I can."

"I appreciate it, Jay, I really do. Not many people—especially coaches in the NFL—have the guts to open up the way you have with me."

"Sean, I gotta run. It's been fun chatting with you about all this. You know where I stand. Whatever you decide to print, I hope it brings you closer to your goals and lands you the job you want."

We shook hands. "Thank you, Jay. And good luck on Sunday."

He nodded. "Think big, win big, baby!"

He turned around and hurried to leave the practice field. Before he left, he had one final piece of advice for me.

34

The sky had turned darker, the practice lights had brightened, and Jay turned back to me one more time as I scribbled notes to summarize our conversation.

"And Sean? One other thing I like to tell my guys. **Whenever you're facing a difficult decision, think of two people facing the same decision and ask yourself, 'What would the bigger person do in this situation?' You'll be amazed how that simple question can focus your mind on what needs to be done.**"

I nodded and waved as Jay Porter exited through the fence gate.

That question haunted me on my drive home and it continued to haunt me as I opened my laptop that evening and gave my article one final read-through.

What would the bigger person do in this situation?

Would the bigger person write a feature loaded with cheap shots and cynicism? Was I acting with integrity and doing what I thought was right or trying to convince myself it was acceptable to do what I knew was wrong? Was I following my heart or chasing a short-term paycheck? Was I taking a risk and daring to do something different or was I conforming to what someone else — someone I didn't even admire — said I should do?

The night before, I had convinced myself I was thinking big by doing what a big-time sports site wanted me to do. Ethan told me this is what I had to do to enter *the big leagues* of sports writing. I didn't make the rules. I had to follow them, right? If I wanted to make it big, to make my big dream come true, I would have to do uncomfortable things, right?

Now, I wasn't so sure.

What would the bigger person do in this situation?

Was writing the column Ethan wanted me to write actually an example of thinking small and short-sighted? Was I so focused on pleasing one particular editor at one particularly snarky sports site that I wasn't seeing the bigger picture of what I wanted my career to look like in the long run? Was this the type of writer I wanted to be? Was this the type of publication I wanted to work for?

What would the bigger person do in this situation?

Why *was* I mocking everything Jay said? He was motivating me to change the way I was thinking. He was inspiring me to think bigger. Did I have an honest change of heart about Jay and his philosophy the night before or was I only trying to appease Ethan? Was it thinking big or small to silence your own morals in order to be popular with the so-called *cool* crowd and do what they said you should do?

What would the bigger person do in this situation?

How would the bigger person respond to this dilemma? Would they silence their inner voice — that voice that kept questioning whether they were being honest and fair — in order to land a job? Would they be so focused on short-term rewards that they sacrificed their own integrity?

What would the bigger person do in this situation?

The question ran through my head as I read through my column and my notes.

That's when it all hit me.

I had spent the last three years thinking small. And here I was doing it again.

I was writing a column I didn't feel good about. I was too focused on the short-term and not thinking of the big picture and the type of writer I ultimately wanted to be.

Jay told me his life changed when he started thinking big about what he wanted to achieve and the type of person he wanted to become. That meant thinking of your biggest dream life and aiming for no less than that.

It was time for me to do the same. What did I really want for myself? What would my dream life look like?

It was time to think big. To take the higher road, do the bigger thing, dream the bigger dream, and expect the bigger success.

I saved my file, closed my document, and grabbed my phone. I texted Ethan: *Sorry for the late notice, just finished another interview with Jay. Got some great quotes and have to add a few things. Story is almost done. Need three more hours to finalize. It will be worth it.*

Less than a minute later, Ethan responded with: *Don't let me down.*

And with that, I drove to a nearby 24-hour diner, put on headphones, and rewrote my entire story.

The bulk of it would remain the same. Practice routines, quotes from players and coaches, even most of Jay's quotes remain untouched. This was still an inside look at how a team spent two weeks preparing for the Super Bowl.

What changed was my commentary throughout the story. Instead of adding cynical rebuttals to Jay's quotes, I let my guard down and revealed how those lessons were impacting me personally, how I saw them impacting the team, and how my skepticism about Jay Porter's philosophy had turned into support for it.

I wrote from the heart, unafraid of how my thoughts might make me look or if I was revealing too much personal information or how the whole story might come across if St. Louis got destroyed on Sunday. I opened up about how Jay was inspiring me to change my own thinking, just as he was doing for his team.

An hour went by like ten minutes as I wrote frantically. I ignored the critical voice in my head and wrote the most honest piece I had ever written, sharing my personal struggles and openly pondering how things could have been different for me over the last three years if I had lived by Jay's teachings.

Three hours went by.

Then four.

Then five.

I kept texting Ethan, assuring him the story was coming.

He knew something was wrong. He was losing his patience. His final text to me read: *This is very unprofessional. I'm not sure we'll be able to work with each other if this is how you do things.*

I imagined how much angrier he was going to be when he read the final piece.

As I wrote, I kept thinking of ways I could eventually expand this column into an entire book. There was so much great advice Jay had given me, much more than I could fit into one online column.

I had never experienced a writing session like this. I was in *the zone* athletes often talk about, losing track of time and no longer hearing that inner voice of self-doubt. It was like that scene in *Jerry Maguire*, where the sports agent has a change of heart and writes through the night as he never has before.

I was putting my entire career on the line as I promised to write from the heart and let the chips fall where they may. Because that's what the bigger person would do. The bigger person would be big enough to handle the fallout, whatever it may be.

Inspired by my last talk with Jay, I even said a little prayer, telling God I would write the truth and trust him with the results.

Shortly after midnight, I finished rereading my piece for the final time.

The last paragraph of my 3,000-word feature read:

I don't know whether the Stallions will win on Sunday. Every expert says they don't have a chance. What I do know is that this team isn't done winning. Not by a long shot. This Super Bowl run is no fluke. The Stallions are in this game for a reason and as long as Jay Porter is their coach, I wouldn't bet against them.

I emailed it to Ethan and texted him that it was sent. It would have been after 2 a.m. on the East Coast, where he was.

I didn't hear back.

I went home. I took a long, hot shower, dropped into bed, and wondered if I'd just thrown away the biggest opportunity of my career.

Part of me hoped Ethan would read it and be moved by my emotional column, decide I was correct to write it the way I did, and hire me anyway, as a voice that could take *The Cheap Seats* in a new direction.

The other part of me knew that was highly unlikely. And I could live with that. I had bigger things in store for my life.

I was thinking beyond one article or one job at one sports site I wasn't even a fan of.

I was thinking bigger.

35

I woke up to the incessant buzzing of my cell phone at 6 a.m.

It was Ethan.

I cleared my throat, took my phone into the hallway, and answered with a groggy, "Ethan, good morning."

"What the hell is this?!" he said, sounding nothing like the charming editor I was used to. "This is not the article we agreed to, not even close."

"I know," I said. "But I thought once you saw it, you'd be pleased with how it turned out. This is the most honest, heartfelt—"

"Pleased?! You thought I'd be *pleased*? You did the exact *opposite* of what I asked you to do. You ignored everything I hired you to do. This whole article makes you sound like a complete amateur. This isn't some small-town paper where people care about your renewed outlook on life. Nobody wants to read a fluff piece about *you*."

"It's a detailed look at how the team has prepared for this moment and how they got here. I added a running commentary with my opinions like you told me to do."

"You know damn well this isn't what I told you to do."

"You want me to take out my opinions?"

"I don't want anything from you ever again. You have burned your bridge with me. You purposely defied what I asked for. You are done. And I'm not paying you a dime for this worthless piece of crap."

"Tell me what you really think."

"Oh, you think this is funny? I should sue you for lying to me and sabotaging my company. I'm the one who got access to the team, and now it's too late, I can't hire anyone else to fix your mess. You ruined it. You wasted this opportunity for us. You said I could depend on you. I knew I never should have worked with you. You are a joke. A small-time joke. I'm going to make sure everyone in this business knows not to work with you. You are finished, Mister Riley. You are done as a sportswriter."

And with that cordial sendoff, Ethan hung up.

36

I walked back into the bedroom and saw Jenny standing by our bed with a worried look.

"What is it?" she said.

"I scrapped the story I showed you. Rewrote the entire piece last night. This time from the heart. I was as honest as I could be."

"And?"

"And Ethan just fired me. He's not going to print it. He's not going to pay me. He sure as hell isn't going to hire me fulltime."

"I'm sorry, Sean." She placed her hand on my back and rubbed lightly. "But you did the right thing."

"I'm not so sure about that," I said, suddenly questioning my bold decision.

"Can I read it?"

"Might as well. You and I are going to be the only people who ever do."

37

I was out back drinking my morning coffee and watching the sunrise when Jenny came to join me after reading my column. She had a smile on her face and tears in her eyes.

"I am so proud of you, Sean. This is the greatest piece you've ever written. I don't care what that jerk says, you did the right thing. You need to shop it to another site."

I shook my head. "It's too late. The game is tomorrow. The whole point was to publish it prior to the game."

"People *need* to read this," she said. "It's inspiring. People need that right now. They need to learn more about a coach like this. We all need more stories like this. Anyone can write a sarcastic piece like your original one. This is different."

"You're so good to me," I said, giving my wife a hug. "I knew this would probably happen. I did it anyway."

"You did the right thing," she said again.

I spent Saturday with my Uber hat back on, driving customers all over the city. One trip after another. I had to make up for the lost pay and find a way to cover my stay in St. Louis, which I was sure Ethan would no longer reimburse me for.

Some of my riders were in town for the Super Bowl. A few were from St. Louis. I couldn't bring myself to share any stories about Jay. I didn't want to explain why my article would never see the light of day.

All afternoon and evening, I held out hope that Ethan would have a change of heart. Maybe someone else on *The Cheap Seats* staff would read the story and convince him this was actually worth publishing.

I never heard anything from him.

As the day went on, I continued to second-guess my decision.

Had I made a mistake? Should I have ignored that pesky inner voice of mine and given Ethan what he wanted? Was I being naive? Did I just throw away the best chance I would ever have of becoming a national sports columnist?

38

On Super Bowl Sunday, Jenny convinced me to use my press pass and go to the game. I told her I needed to earn some money, but she didn't budge. She insisted I take advantage of this once-in-a-lifetime opportunity.

I got there three hours before kickoff. I wanted to take in the sights and sounds of the biggest sporting event on the planet. My press credential allowed me to stand on the Stallions sideline. Jay spotted me during his pregame walk-through.

"I didn't think you were coming," he said with a smile as he shook my hand.

"I couldn't write the article I warned you about," I said. "I wrote from the heart and the new piece got buried. They wanted something controversial. They aren't going to print what I wrote."

"All that work and they're not printing *anything*?"

"It would appear so."

"Something will come of it," he said. "If nothing else, you're here at the Super Bowl, right?"

I nodded. "Thanks, Jay."

I didn't detect any nervous tension from the head coach about to participate in the Super Bowl.

"How are you feeling?" I asked.

"Outstanding. This is going to be a great day."

I smiled and shook my head. "You're not nervous?"

He shrugged. "A little. But the gameplan is in, the preparation is done. We're ready."

He shook my hand again and slapped me on the shoulder. "Gotta run. We'll be seeing you, Sean."

I thanked him again, wished him good luck, and watched one of the greatest Super Bowls ever played from the St. Louis sidelines.

39

I'm sure you know the story. As every Super Bowl tends to be, the game was the most-watched television event of the year.

The upstart St. Louis Stallions, 17.5-point underdogs to the superstar-loaded Cincinnati Bengals, fell behind early. It was 14–0 after the first quarter and it looked like the experts were right; this game was on its way to being one of the most lopsided Super Bowls ever.

Early in the second quarter, starting quarterback Troy Wallace broke off an improvised 36-yard run, which set the team up for a field goal, St. Louis' first points of the game. Cincinnati 14, St. Louis 3.

On Cincinnati's responding drive, the St. Louis defense forced a fumble and recovered it on the Bengals' 33-yard line. The Stallions had life. Maybe this would be a game after all.

Six plays later, Wallace hit wide receiver Myles

Morgan on a fade route for a touchdown from 8 yards out. The ball should have been picked. It was tipped by a Cincinnati defender and somehow ended up in Morgan's hands. Cincinnati 14, St. Louis 10.

The Bengals responded by marching down the field and answering with a quick field goal, extending their lead to 17–10 with seven minutes left in the half.

The teams traded punts, and that's when apparent disaster struck St. Louis.

The Stallions started the drive on their own 6-yard line. On second down, the St. Louis pocket broke down. Wallace took off upfield and was tackled awkwardly a yard short of the first down. He hopped up after the play and immediately went back down. Uh-oh.

He was helped off the field by the trainers, barely able to put pressure on his left foot. A dreaded high-ankle sprain.

Backup quarterback Marshall Lewis entered the game on third and one, deep in his own territory, with less than two minutes left in the half. What a welcome to the biggest stage of his career.

The Bengals had all three timeouts, which meant if Marshall couldn't keep the drive alive, Cincinnati would likely get the ball back with good field position and plenty of time to score again.

Operating out of the shotgun, Marshall took the snap, read the defensive end, and pulled the ball back from running back Jaylin Mack's arms, who was racing right-to-left in front of Marshall. The backup quarterback took a step forward, as though he was going to run it himself, but then pulled up and threw the ball to his wide receiver who was streaking across the field. It was a run-pass-option play, where the quarterback decides whether to give the ball to his running back, keep it on a run himself, or pass the ball downfield. It's a difficult play to execute, requiring the quarterback to make split-second decisions based on how the defense reacts to the play. Marshall chose a pass to his receiver, a decision that proved correct.

His receiver caught the pass in stride 5 yards beyond the line of scrimmage, made one defender miss, turned upfield, and gained 29 yards before he was pushed out of bounds at the St. Louis 44-yard line.

The Stallions were no longer thinking, pick up the first down and keep Cincinnati's offense off the field. They were now thinking, let's score some points before the end of the half.

Marshall led St. Louis down the field on a brilliant drive. He ran the ball twice for 14 yards and completed five of six passes for 71 yards. His last completion occurred with nine seconds left in the half when we fired a 20-yard dart between two defenders and hit his receiver on a seam route for the touchdown.

The game was tied 17–17 at the half. The experts couldn't believe it. Bengals fans were shocked. We had us a ballgame after all.

In the second half, despite the pain of his injury, Troy Wallace returned to the field with a heavily-taped ankle. The two teams battled back and forth.

St. Louis took its first lead of the game with a 48-yard field goal early in the third quarter, 20–17.

Cincinnati answered quickly with a deep touchdown pass to retake the lead, 24–20.

The Stallions punted on their next drive. The Bengals drove down to the St. Louis 32-yard line and attempted a field goal, but a defensive lineman got a hand on the ball and blocked it. It was as though every time Cincinnati looked ready to run away with the game, St. Louis would do something dramatic to stay in it.

Early in the fourth quarter, trailing 24–20, the Stallions were driving down the field when Wallace threw a red-zone interception. It was a brutal turn of events for St. Louis.

On the sidelines, Jay met a devasted Troy Wallace.

"Forget about it," Jay shouted above the roar of the crowd. "There is no problem big enough to stop you. Attack and adapt. We are with you all the way."

Wallace nodded, trying to put the pick behind him. "Six seconds."

On the next drive, Cincinnati converted a crucial fourth-down play near midfield, completed a 24-yard pass two plays letter, and ran the ball into the end zone from 3 yards out to cap the drive.

With half a quarter left, the Bengals led 31–20 and again looked poised to pull away, closer to how all the experts predicted they would.

But St. Louis didn't flinch.

Led by Wallace, the Stallions answered with a fourteen-play drive capped off with a 4-yard touchdown run from Jaylin Mack. St. Louis went for the two-point-conversion and got it when Wallace hit his slot receiver on a creative inside-out route.

The Bengals took over with less than three minutes

to play, leading 31–28. They ran the ball for short gains on first and second down, forcing St. Louis to use its final two timeouts. The Bengals ran the ball again on third down and even though they did not pick up the first down, the play ran the clock down to the two-minute warning. Cincinnati had to punt on fourth down, meaning St. Louis would get one more shot on offense.

After a short punt return, St. Louis took over on its own 28-yard line with 1:51 left in the Super Bowl.

Wallace twice hit his receivers on comeback routes near the sidelines, allowing them to get out of bounds and stop the clock after gains of 7 and 8 yards. With a new set of downs at their own 43-yard line, Wallace was flushed out of the pocket and used his speed to pick up 16 yards, to the Cincinnati 41, where he was tackled in bounds with 1:29 left to play.

The St. Louis offense hurried to the line of scrimmage. Wallace read the defense and changed the play call, the clock still ticking. After the snap, he threw it deep, but overshot his man and the pass fell incomplete. The clock finally stopped with 1:07 left in the game.

A field goal would tie it, but the Stallions needed 6

more yards to feel comfortable with a kick from this distance.

On second down, a Cincinnati defensive lineman deflected Wallace's pass and it fell incomplete.

On third down, Wallace surveyed the field, checked down from left to right, and fired a strike that hit his favorite receiver, Myles Morgan, just past the first-down marker, where he was pushed out of bounds with 55 seconds left to play.

First down Stallions, at the 30.

With a new set of downs, the Stallions were in field-goal range.

On first down, Wallace hit his tight end for a 10-yard gain and another first down.

On the next play, Wallace targeted Morgan in the end zone, but Cincinnati's corner made a great play on the ball and broke up the pass.

On second down from the 20-yard line, St. Louis surprised everyone by running the ball inside. Mack picked up 9 quick yards, but that left the clock running. Now less than 25 seconds left to play. Ball on the 11-yard line.

On third and one, Wallace kept the ball on a zone read play. He picked up the first down, but was tackled in bounds at the 4-yard line.

Clock running as the Stallions rushed to get lined up. 0:13 … 0:12 … 0:11.

Wallace took the snap and spiked the ball, which stopped the clock with 10 seconds left to play.

No timeouts left. Options were limited. A running play could end up running out the clock if it didn't score.

On first down, Wallace threw a pass towards the back corner of the end zone, intended again for Morgan, but the coverage was tight and the pass was too high.

There were now just four seconds left in the game. A field goal would tie it.

But just like he had done against L.A. in the NFC Championship, Jay wasn't playing for overtime. He was going for the win on this final play.

If St. Louis scored, Jay would be viewed a risk-taking genius. If St. Louis failed, he would be called a fool, criticized for not taking the points and sending the game into overtime.

The team lined up in the exact same formation they lined up in for the final play against L.A., a formation which allowed the offensive tackle to be an eligible receiver. Surely, they wouldn't try the same tackle-eligible play again.

Cincinnati called timeout, wanting to make sure everyone on their defense was on the same page.

When St. Louis lined up again, the Stallions were in a completely different formation. The Bengals used their final timeout, again wanting to make sure their defense was ready for all scenarios.

It was cat-and-mouse gamesmanship. Jay had shown two very different formations, knowing the Bengals would have to call timeouts once they saw them.

Finally, with both teams out of timeouts, the St. Louis offense took the field with Wallace at quarterback in the shotgun formation and running back Jaylin Mack lined up to his left and slightly behind him in the backfield. A tight end and wide receiver were also lined up on the left side of the formation. On the right side, one receiver was split out wide and Myles Morgan lined up in the slot position.

The ball was snapped and Morgan sprinted across the field, right to left, in front of Wallace. Cincinnati's defender, playing man coverage, mirrored Morgan step for step on the defensive side. Everyone in the stadium expected Morgan to get the ball.

Everyone except the St. Louis players and coaches.

While Morgan sprinted across the field in front of Wallace, running back Mack ran behind him in the other direction, left to right. Wallace faked a touch pass to Morgan, then sprinted to the right, despite his bum wheel. Mack also sprinted right, about 5 yards wide of and 1 yard behind Wallace.

The Stallions' right side wideout moved upfield and blocked the cornerback in front of him. The St. Louis offensive linemen blocked down on the defenders in front of or to the left of them.

Only Cincinnati's defensive end was left unblocked.

Wallace sprinted towards him, forcing the defensive end to make a decision. He could defend Wallace or he could defend Mack, but he couldn't defend both of them at the same time. It all happened so fast. He chose Wallace, and just a split-second before he hit Wallace at the 3-yard line, Wallace pitched the ball to Mack, who was still running to the right of and about a yard deeper than his quarterback. The nearest Cincinnati safety reacted fast, but not fast enough.

Mack caught the pitch and glided past the goal line for the win.

It was an old-fashioned, college-style speed option play. An ironic message to all those critics who thought Jay Porter and his offense belonged in college.

Jay tossed his headset as high as he could. He and everyone else on the St. Louis sideline rushed the field.

The game was over. St. Louis 34, Cincinnati 31. Jay Porter and the Stallions had pulled off the upset of all upsets.

Journalists aren't supposed to celebrate. But hey, I wasn't working for anyone. And even if I had been, I don't think I could have contained myself.

As the confetti fell, I rushed onto the field, jumping and pumping my fist. I hugged players, coaches, random staff members.

Never in my life had I been so happy after a game.

40

I covered Jay's postgame press conference with all the other reporters, even though I wasn't being paid to do so. I simply didn't want to leave. I wanted to enjoy this moment as long as I could. I stayed in the back and never asked any questions of my own. In all the postgame commotion, I never got to personally congratulate Jay.

I fought two hours of traffic to get home, but I didn't mind. I was too happy to be annoyed. Seeing the Stallions win the way they did made me feel like *I* had won something. As Jay had said prior to the game, this one was for all the underdogs out there.

It felt like more than a game. It was more than the greatest upset in Super Bowl history. It was confirmation that Jay's philosophy was legit. His team *had* overachieved. His team *had* outperformed their talent level. Was it their think-big attitude that made the difference? It sure seemed like it to me.

The victory spoke to me. I had just seen the power of attitude come through on the biggest stage there was. It was time for me to start thinking the same way. No more wavering. What did I have to lose by thinking big? The way I had been thinking the last three years certainly hadn't worked for me.

Yes, I was still broke. Yes, I was still unemployed. Yes, I was still upset I wasn't getting paid for all my work over the past two weeks.

But at that moment, alone in my car on the way home from the Super Bowl, I actually said out loud, "I choose to think big. I am bigger than my problems. Big things are coming my way. I'm choosing to believe it."

Was it cheesy? Sure. Did I feel silly declaring my intentions out loud? Yes, I did. But it felt good. It brought a smile to my face.

Regardless of what I had been through and what I was dealing with at the moment, it was time for a change. It was time to think different. It was time to think big.

"Think big to win big!" I shouted, laughing with joy as I thought of Jay holding the Lombardi Trophy high as confetti fell throughout So-Fi Stadium.

41

An hour before midnight, I received a text from Ethan.

In light of the monumental upset, I have decided to run your story as a post-Super Bowl column. Send me a rewritten final paragraph ASAP.

I sent him the following:

On Sunday evening, St. Louis pulled off the biggest Super Bowl upset of the past half-century. On the biggest stage there is, the Stallions thought big and they won big. There will be plenty of cynics calling this game a fluke and there will be plenty who continue to scoff at Jay Porter's leadership style. But after spending two weeks watching what goes on behind the scenes with Porter's team, I am not about to doubt the power of thinking big. The Stallions won big because they dared to believe big. And as long as Jay Porter is their coach, this reporter believes they're going to continue to win big.

I didn't hear anything else from Ethan, but he did publish my story and he did pay me for it. He never offered me a fulltime job. I wouldn't have accepted it if he did. I was thinking bigger.

The morning after the Super Bowl, Jay texted me and asked me to meet with him before he left town. We met at a coffee shop, the same one where I had met with Marshall Lewis a few days prior.

When I got there, Jay was on his third cup of coffee. His eyes were red, but he still looked like a man standing on top of the world.

I congratulated him, told him that was the greatest game I ever witnessed. He thanked me and told me he was running on less than two hours of sleep, but he was the happiest he'd ever been.

"I couldn't sleep," he said, "so I read your piece this morning. I'm glad they came to their senses and published it. You did a helluva job."

"It was the truth," I said. "Your philosophy is changing the way I think."

"I'm glad to hear that." Jay looked at his watch. "We're about to head out, but I wanted to meet you in person and ask you a question."

"Shoot."

"A few weeks ago, my agent told me I've been offered a book deal. It's a lucrative one."

"That's great, Jay. People need to hear your story. They need to learn your philosophy."

"The thing is, I'm not a writer. I need someone who is to write the book with me."

I almost lost my composure, anticipating what I hoped Jay was about to ask me.

"My question for you, Sean, is if you would be that writer? We can split the money right down the middle. I need someone I trust and after reading what you wrote, I trust you to do the job right."

My eyes filled with water. I raised a fist to my pursed lips, choking back tears as I tried not to cry like a baby. I forced myself to nod several times.

"It would be an honor," I finally said, with a lump in my throat. "You don't know what this means to me."

Jay smiled big and stood up. "It's a deal then. My agent will contact you in the next few days with the details. I'm looking forward to continuing our conversations."

I stood up on wobbly legs. I could not believe this was happening. The opportunity of a lifetime.

"Me too, Jay. Thank you so much."

We hugged and Jay left. For a moment, my legs

wouldn't move. I thought I might be dreaming.

42

In the weeks that followed, Jay made good on his promise. I received my half of the initial book advance — the largest sum of money I had ever seen in my life — and spent a few weeks in St. Louis interviewing Jay, learning more details about his upbringing — a much more difficult childhood than I realized — and more about his family, his mentors, his thoughts on football, and, of course, his life philosophy.

In the spring, I finished the manuscript and sent it to the publisher well before the deadline. The early reviews have been strong and the publisher liked it so much they signed me to a three-book deal for future projects. Hollywood has also shown interest in it, looking to turn Jay's life story into a movie.

My writing style and Jay's endorsement of me has led to several other book opportunities with coaches and athletes.

It isn't lost on me that none of this would have happened had I stuck with the original small-minded, snarky column Ethan had requested from me.

Also in the offseason, Jay signed a five-year contract extension with the St. Louis Stallions. Troy Wallace signed a new contract as well. And even though St. Louis could not afford to keep two top-tier quarterbacks on its roster, Marshall Lewis' game-tying scoring drive at the end of the first half of the Super Bowl proved to the rest of the NFL he was still one of the top QBs in the game. He was traded to the New York Giants and immediately named their starter. (Once he was signed with the Giants, he gave me the green light to share his off-the-record comments publicly.)

On a fall Sunday evening on our back patio, Jenny and I were relaxing with drinks as we watched the Stallions on TV and our kids playing nearby. The camera showed Jay on the sidelines, and I said to Jenny, "That man changed my life. Can you believe where we were a year ago and where we are now? It's all because of that man."

"It could have been much different," she said. "You chose to believe him. You chose to buy into his ideas.

These days, that's not the 'cool' thing to do. You made the decision to change. And I'm so thankful you did."

I took a deep breath, looked at my beautiful wife, and smiled as I raised my glass. "I don't know if I would have done it had you not encouraged me to."

I was so grateful for her. Here I was, living my dream life. But I had almost thrown it away by being short-sighted, by thinking less of what I was capable of, by thinking small.

Jay had dared me to think big. Jenny encouraged me to take the leap. My life changed when I listened to them both.

"You've got to think big to win big," Jenny said.

We clinked our glasses together and watched as Jay led the Stallions to another victory.

About the Author

DARRIN DONNELLY is the bestselling author of *Think Like a Warrior*, *Relentless Optimism*, *The Mental Game*, and several other books in the inspirational *Sports for the Soul* series. Though the main characters in Donnelly's books are usually coaches or athletes, they represent anyone with a big dream and the desire to be successful. The seasons and games they endure represent the seasons of life we all must go through when trying to master a new skill, achieve a new goal, or rebound from a setback.

Sports for the Soul books help readers fill their minds with motivation and positivity while also learning how to build a winner's mindset, overcome adversity, and achieve their goals — in all areas of life.

Donnelly lives in the suburbs of Kansas City with his wife and three children.

He can be reached at *SportsForTheSoul.com* and on X/Twitter *@DarrinDonnelly*.

Sports for the Soul®

Books That Motivate, Inspire, and Empower.

This book is part of the *Sports for the Soul* series. For updates on this book, future books, and a free newsletter that delivers advice and inspiration from top coaches, athletes, and sports psychologists, join us at: **SportsForTheSoul.com**.

The *Sports for the Soul* newsletter will help you:

- Find your calling and follow your passion
- Harness the power of positive thinking
- Build your self-confidence
- Attack every day with joy and enthusiasm
- Develop mental toughness
- Increase your energy and stay motivated
- Explore the spiritual side of success
- Be a positive leader for your family and your team
- And much more…

Join us at: **SportsForTheSoul.com**.

Don't miss the previous books in the *Sports for the Soul* series...

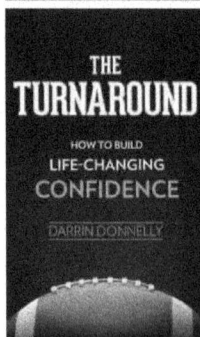

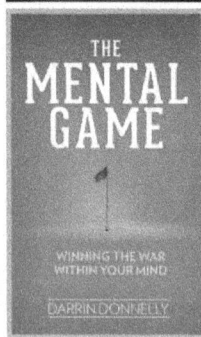

THINK LIKE A
WARRIOR
THE FIVE
INNER BELIEFS
THAT MAKE YOU
UNSTOPPABLE

DARRIN DONNELLY

OLD SCHOOL
GRIT
TIMES MAY CHANGE
BUT THE RULES FOR
SUCCESS
NEVER DO

DARRIN DONNELLY

RELENTLESS
OPTIMISM
HOW A
COMMITMENT TO
POSITIVE THINKING
CHANGES EVERYTHING

DARRIN DONNELLY

LIFE
to the
FULLEST
A STORY ABOUT
FINDING YOUR PURPOSE
AND FOLLOWING YOUR HEART

DARRIN DONNELLY

VICTORY
FAVORS THE
FEARLESS
HOW TO
DEFEAT THE 7 FEARS
THAT HOLD YOU BACK

DARRIN DONNELLY

THE
TURNAROUND
HOW TO BUILD
LIFE-CHANGING
CONFIDENCE

DARRIN DONNELLY

THE
MENTAL
GAME
WINNING THE WAR
WITHIN YOUR MIND

DARRIN DONNELLY

For more information, visit SportsForTheSoul.com

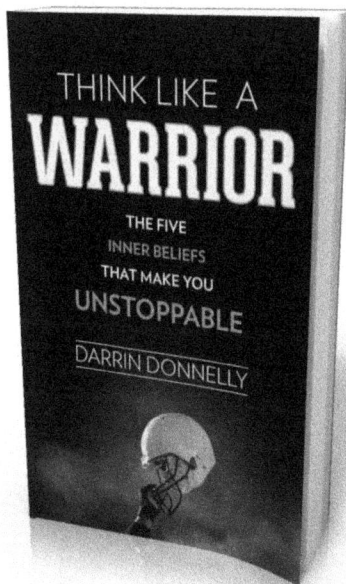

Think Like a Warrior

by Darrin Donnelly

In this bestselling inspirational fable, a college football coach at the end of his rope receives mysterious visits from five of history's greatest coaches: **John Wooden, Buck O'Neil, Herb Brooks, Bear Bryant, and Vince Lombardi.** Together, these legendary leaders teach him the five inner beliefs shared by the world's most successful people. The "warrior mindset" he develops changes his life forever — and it will change yours as well.

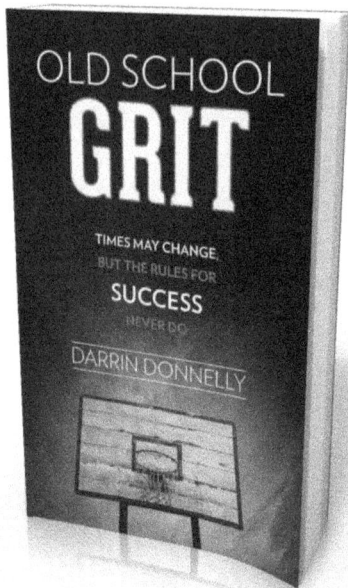

Old School Grit

by Darrin Donnelly

An old-school college basketball coach who thinks like John Wooden and talks like Mike Ditka enters the final NCAA tournament of his legendary career and uses his last days as a coach to write letters to the next generation revealing his rules for a happy and successful life: the 15 rules of grit. Consider this book an instruction manual for getting back to the values that truly lead to success and developing the type of old school grit that will get you through anything.

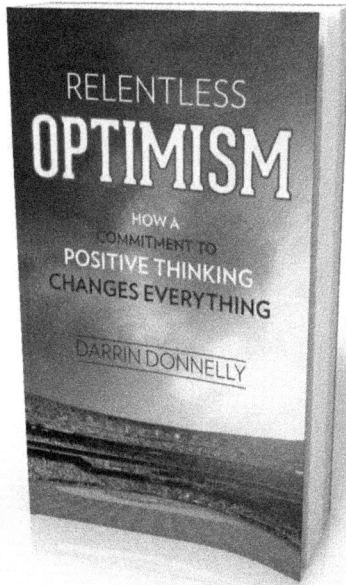

Relentless Optimism

by Darrin Donnelly

A minor-league baseball player realizes his lifelong dream of making it to the majors is finally coming to an end. That is, until he meets an unconventional manager who teaches him that if he wants to change his outcomes in life, he must first change his attitude. This book will show you just how powerful a positive attitude can be and it will teach you how to use positive thinking to make your biggest dreams come true.

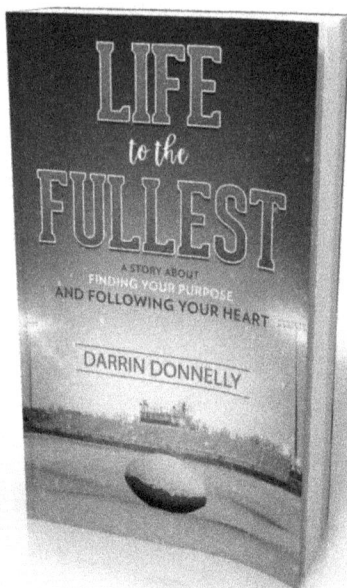

Life to the Fullest

by Darrin Donnelly

This is an inspirational football fable for anyone who has ever struggled to find their purpose or questioned whether it was safe to follow their passion in life. It's a story about fathers and sons. It's a story about faith, family, and community. Most of all, it's a story about having the courage to follow your heart and live your true purpose.

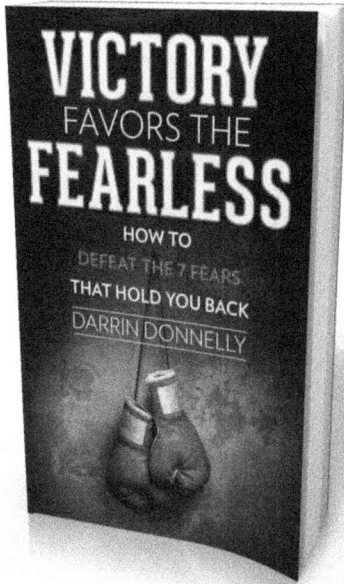

Victory Favors the Fearless

by Darrin Donnelly

A struggling pro boxer learns from a wise trainer that he'll never defeat his opponents in the ring until he first defeats the fears within himself. As this fighter learns to defeat the seven common fears that hold him back, it propels him on a journey that takes him all the way to a championship battle for the ages.

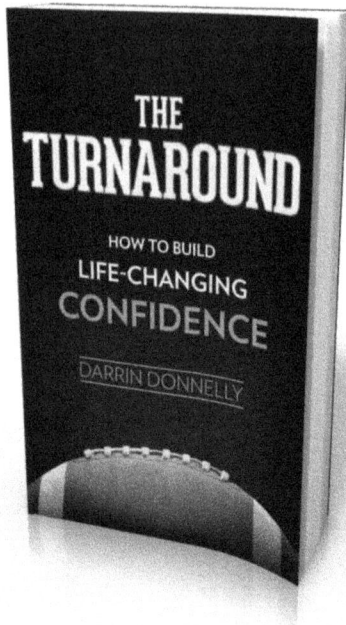

The Turnaround
by Darrin Donnelly

Danny O'Connor is an insecure fourth-string quarterback on one of the worst college football teams in America. But his life changes when a new coach is hired and begins showing Danny and his teammates how to build the confidence needed to turn around their losing ways. As this story plays out, you will learn the practical, real-world methods used by some of the greatest coaches of all time for instantly generating self-confidence.

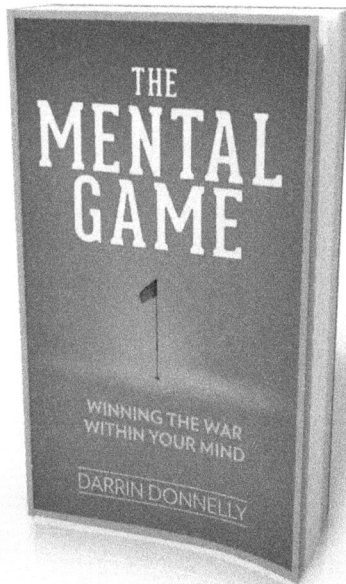

The Mental Game

by Darrin Donnelly

Jack McKee is a professional golfer ready to quit on his dream after years of struggle and an embarrassing public meltdown. In an attempt to figure out why his career has ended up the way it has, Jack reaches out to one of the game's greatest former players for advice. This legendary golfer teaches Jack that the problem is not in his swing, but in his mind. This book is about winning the mental game we all must play on a daily basis.

www.ingramcontent.com/pod-product-compliance
Lightning Source LLC
Chambersburg PA
CBHW030822090426
42737CB00009B/828